PRAISE FOR *CITY ON A HILL*

Kyle Schwahn makes a key contribution to the gospel-centered movement by demonstrating how a robust understanding of the biblical gospel stimulates and shapes the spiritual vitality of a congregation, which in turn adds credibility to its witness to the world as the church matures into Christ-likeness. This book will be valuable both to his fellow pastors and to church members who would benefit from a fresh appreciation of this vital connection between the gospel preached and the gospel practiced, both individually and corporately.

Randy Roberts, President/Professor of Christian Spirituality, Western Seminary (Portland, OR)

Schwahn's thoughtfulness and care in applying the ethic of love and the truth of the gospel to everyday life in the church is refreshing, encouraging, and a needed challenge for local expressions of Christ's body. *City on a Hill* proves thoroughly biblical, easily accessible, and eminently applicable... all the while faithfully exalting Christ from beginning to end.

Dustin Hall, Pastor, Kennewick Baptist Church, President, Northwest Baptist Convention

I have always enjoyed Kyle's skill as a shepherd and teacher, and here you have in your hands where he is guiding his church. I recommend this book to you wholeheartedly, knowing that what you read is an outworking of how he lives and serves those God has entrusted to him.

Darren Carlson, President, Training Leaders International

CITY ON A HILL

THE LIGHT OF CHRIST IN THE LIFE OF HIS CHURCH

Kyle Schwahn

City on a Hill
The Light of Christ in the Life of His Church

© 2019 Kyle Schwahn

Front cover image by Dan Absalonson

ISBN: 978-0-578-50553-4

To Indian Trail Church, for being a living picture of the principles of God's word.

CONTENTS

FOREWORD

You are holding an important book on the priority of love. Some will look at this and think, "I don't need this. I already know about love. I need the deeper truths." But love is the deeper truth, and if you think you have already mastered it, this is a sure sign that you probably haven't. It means you either don't understand God's love, you are completely apathetic about growing in love, or you are so arrogant that you think you have already arrived.

Only those who really understand love know how little they practice it. Where do we obtain an understanding of God's love? The gospel is God's classroom. There we see a spiritual love that "surpasses knowledge" (Eph. 3:19).

In these pages my friend, Kyle Schwahn, will show you that the church exists to glorify God, and that nothing brings praise, honor, and glory to God like a community of Christians growing in their capacity to love. This book will also center your understanding of love in the gospel. The gospel helps us grow in love, and it does that in four ways.

First, the gospel shows us what love looks like. It's not a feeling. It is an action. Love pulls up its overalls, puts on its hard hat, and goes to work. In the gospel Jesus suffers for our happiness. Christ performs a love exchange. He takes our sins and pains upon Himself in order to give us His eternal joy and happiness.

Second, the gospel motivates us to attempt this love. It does this by demonstrating God's love, grace, and mercy toward unworthy sinners, and gratitude overwhelms us. Through the gospel we see the beauty of God's goodness and long to imitate it.

Third, the gospel imparts hope. Christ died for my sins and failings. He atoned for my lack of perfection, and therefore I am freed from the burden to be perfect. Because he will always love and forgive me, despite my failings, I can keep striving for the upward call of God in Christ Jesus.

Lastly, the gospel provides power for change. Jesus ascended into heaven to send the Holy Spirit. Without him we cannot love aright. But he indwells God's children, and as the Spirit of love, he enlightens us about the gospel and what it says about love. The result is growth.

Dear reader, is any virtue more sorely needed? Love is the aroma of heaven. Someday we will be perfected in love. "When he appears we shall be like him because we shall see him as he is" (1 John 3:2). That is our hope. That is our inheritance. Until then we will need Kyle Schwahn's book.

I don't know about you, but I have some growing to do. I need to grow in love. My family needs to grow in love. My church needs to grow in love. That means we all need this book (and others like it). I trust you feel the same way.

William P. Farley,
Author of *Gospel Powered Parenting*,
September 2018

INTRODUCTION

EPHESIANS 3:21
to him be glory in the church and in Christ Jesus
throughout all generations, forever and ever. Amen.

When I was fifteen, I went through the American rite of passage known as driver's ed. Each week three of us would pile into a Chevy Corsica with our under-enthusiastic instructor for another driving challenge. One week we had to master the gentle neighborhood streets. Then we moved on to the arterials. Soon came the freeway. And then finally—the last significant milestone—parallel parking.

The parking itself didn't make for a memorable day. Mangled orange cones bore witness to our trouble, but we expected it. We each took our turn and struggled on. But as the third member of our group finished, I witnessed a unique breakthrough moment.

Jenny talked with a friend and me following our drive. Thoroughly confused as to why she couldn't get her parallel parking right, she asked us for help. As young men who had recently succeeded with only one crushed cone, we inflated our chests and began to wax eloquent about the subtler points of geometry. As she listened, she held her hands up as if holding an imaginary steering wheel.

Turning them side to side in front of her she said in frustration, "But that doesn't make sense!" We patiently went over it with her again, but confusion remained. Then came the moment of breakthrough. Her eyes lit up as she blurted out, "Oh, you steer with the *front wheels?* I thought it was the back wheels!"

I share this story not because I'm concerned about the state of driver's ed nowadays (though, if you're an instructor, you may consider a "which wheels steer the car" lesson near the front end of the course). I share it because twice in my Christian life God has graciously given me the same type of *front wheels* moment. In two essential areas of Christian life and ministry, God allowed pieces of His truth to click together in a way which not only made sense but made an impact.

The first breakthrough had to do with the gospel. At the time, I had been a Christian for years and even served in pastoral ministry. If you would've asked me about the gospel, I could've no doubt told you of its importance. I believed in the sinfulness of man and the need for the cross. I knew that Christ's death and resurrection provide the only hope of eternal life. And I had often preached that sinners need to repent and trust in Christ for salvation. This was foundational. It was critical. And it was *initial*.

Although utterly committed to the saving gospel, I didn't see much use for it beyond salvation. To me, it was the *initial* message. The gospel ushered a person into reconciliation with God and a righteous standing with Him. It stood as the entryway into forgiveness and eternal life. But the *initial* truth was only needed for the *initial* step. Once a person came to Christ, they had much more to learn! A Christian needed to know God's truth about holiness, humility, forgiveness, spiritual disciplines and missions. The list could go on. I was glad to give the gospel to unconverted folks. But believers had far too much to master to get bogged down by that *initial* message.

But then, in grace, God gave me my first *front wheels* experience. I had gone to my seminary campus for a week-long intensive course on preaching. But the class wasn't really about how to preach. Our instructor labored to teach us what to preach. And maybe a bit more accurately, *whom* to preach.

Hour after hour and day after day, the professor argued that preachers had been called to proclaim Christ. The gospel of Jesus Christ (the good news of all God accomplished through Him) is central not only to the salvation of a sinner but also to the sanctification of a saint. With more spiritual weight than I could've imagined, that reality came home to my heart. I had always been committed to the gospel, but I had never centered my life and ministry on it.

That week I learned how the gospel serves as the power and pattern of the entire Christian life. The moral imperatives of the Bible don't merely give self-improvement goals for our futures. They exhort us based on what Christ has accomplished. God has always rooted His commands in the soil of redemption.

What God calls Christians to do and be finds root in who He is and what He's done for us. In other words, the triumph of the gospel pulsates as the heartbeat of the entire Christian life. That week I felt as if scales fell from my eyes minute by minute and scripture by scripture. I saw clearly now, and my life and ministry would never be the same.

For years following, I preached Christ as faithfully as I could. People seemed to grow in maturity, and my church grew deeper and deeper in the gospel. I couldn't have imagined God had yet another *front wheels* experience in store for me. This one came as I traveled with some fellow pastors to a church across the country.

The goal for the week was to sit in with another pastoral team as they worked with their congregation. We observed elder meetings, Sunday worship, adult education, members' meetings and more.

Our hosts had scheduled sections of teaching for us between all of those church-life events. They spoke to us about the biblical convictions which undergirded the practices we saw. They taught us about membership, church discipline, discipling and raising up new leaders. It all excited me. But the way God began to work in my heart ran deeper still.

The shift didn't come merely from what I had learned during the weekend, but in what I had experienced. I saw a church striving intentionally for the culture of love and care the New Testament so often spoke of. Their brotherly love evidenced itself in mutual commitment and a shepherding heart. The pastors' love for their people inspired me, and the devotion to intentional discipling thrilled me. My mind began to run through New Testament books and verses. This is what they described! I had always read about these things... but to see them in living color was life-giving.

At one point near the end of the week, a room full of pastors gathered together to share highlights from what they had learned. One of them stood and said, "It's as if you're equipping the *people* to do the work of ministry." The host pastor politely said, "Well, brother, haven't you ever read that in the Bible? That's simply what Ephesians 4 says." The man's response captured my heart completely. He said in a quiet tone, "Yes, but I guess I've just never *seen* it." Once again God had graciously pointed out that the front wheels steer the car.

I filled the days and weeks following my second front wheels moment with frantic activity and study. Gathering with other elders in my church, we searched the New Testament asking, "What do we see about the church... the people of God and their life together?" We wanted to know how God called His church to live together and love and serve one another. I wanted to know if what I had seen and heard was indeed what God Himself had revealed as His desire for the body of Christ.

For weeks I read the scriptures, often slapping my forehead and thinking, of course. What resulted from those weeks of study has become the book you hold. This work represents a collision course between those two front wheels moments in my heart and life: 1) The centrality of the gospel and 2) the church's life of intentional love.

God designed the life of the local church to manifest His glory. In these pages we'll see the centrality of love to the community of faith. We'll see how the gospel empowers the love Jesus called us to. We will consider how the church can walk in unity and purity, and why God intended the structure and gatherings of His church to foster Christ-centered love. We will—I pray—see a vision of the church as the mechanism for the growth and maturity of every believer. In short, we'll see how God intends for His church to love, and so display His glory.

CHAPTER 1

LOVE COMMANDED

1 JOHN 4:11

Beloved, if God so loved us, we also ought to love one another.

His disciples could barely carry him to the church gathering. Old age had taken its toll, not only on his body, but also on his voice. Although accustomed to teaching, he had grown so weak he could scarcely muster the words to address them. But whenever able, the aged apostle John echoed the words of his Master, "Little children, love one another." Although some tired of the elderly disciple exhorting them repeatedly with the same command, John merely sought to pass on what his Lord entrusted to him all those decades before.[1]

On Jesus' last night with His disciples, He gave them a moral vision which would characterize His church: "A new commandment I give to you, that you love one another: just as I have loved you, you also are to love one another. By this all people will know that you are my disciples, if you have love for one another" (John 13:34-35). Jesus' words reoriented the lives of His disciples. If obeyed, His command would leave nothing untouched. In fact, His command would reverberate through the apostles' writings and shape His church throughout history. We still feel the effects of His command today. And we ought to.

I'm writing this book—in large part—about love. I realize that speaking about love has its challenges. Our culture has taken to using the word *love* in ways inconsistent with the command of Christ. Often over-emotionalized, our culture's view of love focuses on subjective feeling. Although feeling isn't absent from Biblical love, it doesn't define it. As Thabiti Anyabwile wrote, "When the Bible speaks of love, it is not referring primarily to some inner feeling but to a gritty and dynamic movement. Love wears work clothes."[2] Our culture also traps us into treating love too commonly. We dilute the meaning of love speaking in one breath to a spouse, "I love you, sweetheart," and in the next of a football team, "I love the Cowboys." Does the love which Jesus commanded have more direction? More depth? Is there anything distinctive about Christian love?

God calls for love *from* His people because it's what He's given *to* His people. Our love follows the pattern of God's love for us. He didn't love us while we were attractive and worthy, but while we were rebellious wretches. Paul clarifies this when he explains, "But God shows his love for us in that while we were still sinners, Christ died for us" (Romans 5:8). The basis for Biblical love doesn't lie in the worthiness of the one loved, but in will of the one loving. The love God lavished on His children—and then calls them to reflect— is a love of choice, not feeling.

LOVE'S ROOTS

The command to love one's neighbor was firmly rooted in Old Testament theology. Upon bringing the nation of Israel out of Egypt and to Mount Sinai, God commanded them to love in two distinct situations. First, He warned them not to take vengeance on one another, but to love their neighbors as themselves (Leviticus 19:18). A little later, He applied the command to sojourners in the land. The Israelites should not take advantage of the vulnerable merely because of their weakness and need. Rather, they should extend the same kind of care and concern that other Israelites enjoyed.

As Jesus taught His disciples—and answered His challengers—He interpreted and applied the Leviticus command more broadly than ever. He presented love as indispensable in obeying all of God's commands. Jesus replied to the Pharisee's question about the greatest commandment saying, "You shall love the Lord your God with all your heart and with all your soul and with all your mind. This is the great and first commandment. And a second is like it: You shall love your neighbor as yourself. On these two commandments depend all the Law and the Prophets" (Matthew 22:37-40).

In saying the law and the prophets *depend* on the commands to love God and neighbor, Jesus used a technical phrase to speak of the law's ideological ancestry[3]. Like the headwaters of a great river, Israel could trace its moral code back to these two main concerns. Elevating love for God and neighbor didn't demean the rest of the laws; in fact, it explained them. Even the Ten Commandments—which served as the centerpiece of Israel's covenantal relationship[4]—aligned with these two loves. Prohibitions against both false worship and taking the Lord's name in vain served as a means of loving God. Injunctions against murder, adultery, theft and coveting simply called God's people to love one another. For Jesus, the kernel of the law lay in these two loves. The Apostle Paul would later pick up on the connection saying, "For the whole law is fulfilled in one word: 'You shall love your neighbor as yourself'" (Galatians 5:14).

The prophets later indicted Israel for failing on both accounts. Generations of Israelites forsook God and one another. As Isaiah confronted Israel for their outward shows of religiosity, he painted a gloomy picture of their failures,

> Is not this the fast that I choose: to loose the bonds of wickedness, to undo the straps of the yoke, to let the oppressed go free, and to break every yoke? Is it not to share your bread with the hungry and bring the homeless poor into your house; when you see the naked, to cover him, and not to hide yourself from your own flesh? (Isaiah 58:6-7)

The prophets rebuked the nation and called them to repentance. They sought to win the people back to obedience to the law they'd received from the beginning. And that law had always been a law of love.

The command to love was firmly rooted in the Old Testament. But if that's the case, then why was Jesus' command to His disciples so important? If the command to love others made up part of Israel's life for generations, why was Jesus' exhortation so revolutionary? And how could He say it was *new*?

LOVE'S NEW REALITY

The night Jesus was betrayed, He gave His disciples a command new in scope. "A new commandment I give to you, that you love one another: just as I have loved you, you also are to love one another. By this all people will know that you are my disciples, if you have love for one another" (John 13:34-35). Commenting on Christ's words, Leon Morris says, "Jesus is not speaking here of love to all people but of love within the community of believers."[5] The "one another" referred to those who left everything to follow Jesus. He gave the command to His disciples so they would love His disciples.

I don't mean to imply that Christians cannot, or should not love those outside of the community of faith. They have. They do. And they will. But Jesus requires us to look at other disciples with a particular brand of care and concern. We must not forsake our brothers and sisters in the faith. In other words, Jesus commanded love with a compass. And other Christians stand at true North. Though we may love others, we must love fellow disciples.

The love command also laid a new pattern. The standard of comparison for His disciples' love is the love of Christ for His disciples. He called them to love as He loved them. Don't miss the timing of His command. Jesus spoke in the shadow of His cross. Perhaps only hours after uttering these words, the betrayal of Judas sent Jesus to His passion. He was given up, flogged and crucified in the place of guilty sinners. On the cross, Jesus displayed His self-sacrificing love. He bore God's curse that He might grant God's blessings. Repeating the love command in the context of His impending death, Jesus said, "This is my commandment, that you love one another as I have loved you. Greater love has no one than this, that someone lay down his life for his friends" (John 5:12-13). The love Jesus commands is new not because it cares for others, but because it does so at high cost. Our cruciform love shows the nature of the gospel as it's expressed.

Jesus' command was new in its scope and pattern. But it also carried with it a new potential result. As people see Christian love, they'll see something in the disciples which proves they belong to Jesus. The watching world will experience the character of Christ through His people. A disciple of Jesus' day followed his teacher to learn. But he didn't seek to learn facts, principles or theology alone. He learned to be transformed. The disciple not only followed his teacher to learn what he knew, but he also to become what he was. After all, "A disciple is not above his teacher, but everyone when he is fully trained *will be like his teacher*" (Luke 6:40, italics mine). The self-sacrificial love of Christ's people will bear witness to Christ by its very existence. D.A Carson writes, "It is a privilege which, rightly lived out, proclaims the true God before a watching world. That is why Jesus ends his injunction with the words, 'All men will know that you are my disciples, if you love one another'".[6]

Our love for one another focuses on the disciples of Christ, follows the pattern of Christ, and bears witness to the character of Christ. This is the new commandment.

LOVE'S REINFORCEMENTS

The disciples who first received the new commandment didn't keep it to themselves. Nor did they live it out by themselves. The unfolding of the New Testament shows Christ's disciples assembled as local churches. Whether in Jerusalem (Acts 2:42), Antioch (Acts 11:21-26), or Lystra and Iconium (Acts 14:21-23), disciples formed congregations committed to one another and to the Lord. The church became the setting in which the ripples of Christ's command would roll out. In fact, much of what the apostles taught about Christ's love command, churches merely fleshed out in practical terms. To quote

Carson again, "This commandment is presented as the marching order for the newly gathering messianic community."[7]

As he wrote to local congregations, Paul praised them for the love they displayed,

> "For this reason, because I have heard of your faith in the Lord Jesus and your love toward all the saints, I do not cease to give thanks for you, remembering you in my prayers" (Ephesians 1:15).

> "We ought always to give thanks to God for you, brothers, as is right, because your faith is growing abundantly, and the love of every one of you for one another is increasing" (2 Thessalonians 1:3).

He also pleaded with God for love to continue to flourish.

> "And it is my prayer that your love may abound more and more, with knowledge and all discernment" (Philippians 1:9).

Paul understood what Jesus commanded. Disciples should love one another. And because love authenticates true discipleship, he praised God when he saw it and prayed it would continue to develop and characterize the life of the church.

But the New Testament writers didn't merely praise and pray for love. They also passed on and applied the command of the Lord. Jesus' love command took center stage in their ethical vision.

> "Now concerning brotherly love you have no need for anyone to write to you, for you yourselves have been

taught by God to love one another, for that indeed is what you are doing to all the brothers throughout Macedonia. But we urge you, brothers, to do this more and more" (1 Thessalonians 4:9-10).

Paul told the Romans to recognize the ever-outstanding "debt" of love (Romans 13:8). In other words, Christians never stop owing love to one another. We have a glorious obligation to love in light of Christ's endless love for us.

To the Corinthians, Paul wrote an entire chapter on the nature and importance of love (1 Corinthians 13). You might recognize the central section:

"Love is patient and kind; love does not envy or boast; it is not arrogant or rude. It does not insist on its own way; it is not irritable or resentful; it does not rejoice at wrongdoing, but rejoices with the truth. Love bears all things, believes all things, hopes all things, endures all things" (1 Corinthians 13:4-7).

Though often used out of context as a preamble to the unity candle, the passage initially regulated life in the body of Christ. God empowered the Corinthians to serve one another. But Paul wanted them to understand that whenever God gives gifts or empowers us for service, He gives so that we might build others up in love. Without love, the gifts are meaningless, and so are those who employ them (1 Corinthians 13:1-3).

Peter urged Christians to obey Jesus' command, "Having purified your souls by your obedience to the truth for a sincere brotherly love, love one another earnestly from a pure heart" (1 Peter 1:22). God not only saved us *from* something. He also saved us to something—a faithful love for other Christians. Later in Peter's letter, his concern for love rises to the surface again, "*Above all,* keep loving one another earnestly" (1 Peter 4:8, italics mine). Above all? Really? Love should trump mutual encouragement or forgiveness? Love should come before compassion and kindness? What about humility and grace? Yes! We pursue love above all because it's the headwaters to all. In fact, in speaking of things like compassion, kindness, humility, meekness, patience, and forgiveness, Paul sums up with this, "And above all these put on love, which binds everything together in perfect harmony" (Colossians 3:14).

The Apostle John held Jesus' love command as a guiding principle for God's people. He wrote, "For this is the message that you have heard from the beginning, that we should love one another" (1 John 3:11). They had heard it from the beginning the night of Jesus' betrayal. John went on to apply the command in specific ways, but his teachings were not innovative. They merely demonstrated how the love Jesus commanded works itself out in the community of faith.

That night in the upper room, Jesus forged a new identity for His disciples. Their love for one another would turn them into a community of light for the nations. The new commandment would bind them together in mutual care, affection and sacrifice to continually show forth the gospel of God's grace. They would be taught and exhorted to love. They would be rebuked when love was absent. And they would be praised when it overflowed among them. This love was part and parcel with being the church because it was a reflection of the One who—in love—purchased the church by His precious blood.

LOVE'S SHAPE

If you've ever seen a famous sculpture, you've likely marveled at the detail and intricacy. It's incredible to think about a man with nothing but a hammer and chisel standing before a massive piece of marble and bringing forth such beauty. But each small blow shapes an unformed mass into a specific image. What emerges is not the mass of rock but the real vision of the artist.

When we think of the love command of Jesus, we ought to view it as a massive but formless piece of marble. Although Jesus gave a specific scope, pattern, and result to this command, He didn't give much detail. Instead, His apostles would later wield their chisels, writing to local churches about the specifics. The apostles wrote to teach what the life of obedient, cruciform love should look like in a congregation of saints. With each stroke of the pen, churches saw more and more of what Christ intended for them. Writing about the calling church members have to one another, John Hammett writes, "In relationships with one another, they carry out these commands in dozens if not hundreds of specific ways, but it could be argued that all the one-another commands are simply expansions on or expressions of the command to love one another."[8]

For instance, when Paul addresses disputable matters—things like eating food sacrificed to idols, or observing certain holy days—he calls upon church members at Rome never to put a stumbling block in front of a brother or sister in Christ. Why? "For if your brother is grieved by what you eat, *you are no longer walking in love*" (Romans 14:15a, italics mine). In other words, Paul shapes the rock of love in regard to issues of disagreement and individual conviction. In Galatians, he takes up the chisel with regard to service. Our new found freedom in Christ should not give opportunity for the flesh and sinful patterns. Rather, "Through love serve one another" (Galatians 5:13b). Practical service to the body expresses the love Jesus called us to. Yet another blow comes in Philippians where Paul calls believers to look not only to their own interests, but to those of others—doing nothing from rivalry or conceit. But Paul roots the call in a greater concern, "Complete my joy by being of the same mind, *having the same love*, being in full accord and of one mind" (Philippians 2:2, italics mine). We've already seen Paul's words to the Colossians in which the rock of love binds together qualities like compassion, kindness, humility, meekness and patience—among others. With each letter the apostles shaped the mass of love into the true vision of God.

CONCLUSION

Throughout the Bible God clearly called His people to love. In both the Old and New Testaments, love takes center stage as the guiding principle for relational harmony. Jesus' teaching sharpened the focus of the call. For His followers' love would focus on other disciples, follow the pattern of Jesus' own self-giving sacrifice, and display the nature of true discipleship. The apostles followed suit, firmly placing the call to love at the center of the church's corporate life. They shaped the calling to love with their letters, leaving the church a rich ethical vision for all of life.

Some of the disciples chafed at the aged Apostle John. Whenever he'd gather with them, he repeated it yet again, "Little children, love one another." Finally, someone asked him "Teacher, why do you always say this?" Perhaps they imagined John's age had gotten the best of him. Maybe the old man had forgotten he'd exhorted them with the phrase over and over again. Or did they simply want to move on to the deeper things of the Christian life? John's answer cut through any remaining doubt, "Because it is the Lord's commandment and if it alone is kept, it is sufficient."[9]

CHAPTER 2

LOVE DEFINED
(LOVE LIKE FAMILY)

1 PETER 1:22
Having purified your souls by your obedience
to the truth for a sincere brotherly love, love
one another earnestly from a pure heart

He received the call from across an ocean and thirteen hours' worth of time zones. His sister's voice on the other end said, "Mom and dad have been in an accident." Within hours, my friend—serving as a missionary in Indonesia—began to travel home to the States. A vehicle collision sent both of his parents to separate hospitals. At the time of the call, he didn't know how serious it was. But he did know he was going to get to his family. It didn't matter that the journey required multiple flights—expensive ones at that. It didn't matter that he'd need to make the trip without his wife and young kids. It didn't matter that he had no car, or place to stay when he landed. What mattered was family. And so he flew.

We respond uniquely to our natural families. We cross barriers and overcome difficulties. Blood is thicker than water, they say. Because family commitment is so ingrained in us all, the New Testament authors employ it as a model for love within the body of Christ. It makes a great deal of sense, doesn't it? As we've seen, God has purified us for *brotherly* love. He's adopted us as sons and daughters through faith in Christ. He's formed us into a new *race* of people—a spiritual kinship (1 Peter 2:9). And although not bound together by physical bloodlines, we are united by the precious blood of Christ. This connection not only binds us in spiritual reality, but also moves us to practical commitment.

I've had many friends over the years who've adopted children. In each case a moment came when a judge's stamp rendered the child a legal part of the new family. The adopted child has new parents, to be sure. But for this reason, he also has new siblings. The same holds true for the adopted children of God. Our common adoptive Heavenly Father makes it appropriate—even imperative—that we see one another as family. Salvation brings us into God's blessing as well as His household.

Paul wrote to the church in Thessalonica saying, "Now concerning brotherly love you have no need for anyone to write to you, for you yourselves have been taught by God to love one another, for that indeed is what you are doing to all the brothers throughout Macedonia. But we urge you, brothers, to do this more and more" (1 Thessalonians 4:9-10). God teaches His new children how to act within the family and how to act like family. But don't miss the appeal. Love should increase more and more. Every local church should steadily deepen its practical, familial care of one another. As the author of Hebrews says, "Let broth-erly love continue" (Hebrews 13:1).

Brotherly love binds us like family even in the face of differences. Church members love one another not because they hold char-acteristics in common, but because they hold Christ in common. Because we share in Christ by faith, the barriers that once divided us can no longer hinder our love. Christians constitute a spiritual family even though they come from different backgrounds, eth-nicities or socio-economic classes. In spite of age and stage of life, they're held together by the gospel. As Paul taught the Galatian church, "There is neither Jew nor Greek, there is neither slave nor free, there is no male and female, for you are all one in Christ Jesus. And if you are Christ's, then you are Abraham's offspring, heirs according to promise" (Galatians 3:28-29). The old walls have come down. A new heritage has taken hold. We now bind ourselves to brothers and sisters who are outwardly unlike us recognizing they are inwardly just like us. We stand as fellow sinners in God's presence saying, "See what kind of love the Father has given to us, that we should be called the children of God" (1 John 3:1).

God designed brotherly love as a direct result of our salvation. And He commands this family-style love within His body. But how does a spiritual family look? If you want to carry out brotherly love faithfully, what things should you do? How will you treat other members of your church?

I'm convinced the Biblical answers to these questions are both normal and natural. We love spiritual family by extending care, offering hospitality and showing genuine affection.

EXTENDING CARE

I began this chapter with the story of my missionary friend's journey to the States because I believe we intuitively know how we would respond in such a situation. When a family faces hardships and burdens, its members rally to provide support and care to one another. I imagine some of you came from dysfunctional families. You don't expect your family to spring into action in the midst of crisis. You've seen them fail to offer care during hard times. But may I humbly suggest that their lack of practical support and care *defines* the dysfunction? A family *ought* to act in these ways.

The New Testament authors utilize family language on this basis. They believe we have an innate understanding of kinship responsibility. And so they transfer that knowledge to the spiritual realm. Caring is what families do.

The mutual care and concern called for among the church expresses itself in both good times and bad. Paul taught the Corinthian church they comprised one body. God sovereignly arranged unique individuals within the church so the church might have the same care for one another (1 Corinthians 12:24-25). That may seem a bit backward to you. If God wanted the same care for all in the body, why didn't He make them all the same? The passage first pictures the body as composed of many different parts. Each part is necessary for the whole to function properly. Therefore, we offer the same care to every part of the body. Every member is vital to health and growth. All are indispensable to the proper function of the church, so, we ought to care for all. But how?

In the same section Paul says, "If one member suffers, all suffer together; if one member is honored, all rejoice together" (1 Corinthians 12:26). When I was about 20 years old, I dislocated a rib. I had never known how interconnected my body parts were until that day! How could one rib make my legs and head hurt at the same time? My whole body felt the pain of one part—no matter how I might've taken it for granted. The same holds true for feelings of pleasure. If I buy my wife a foot massage for Mothers' Day, I know she'll come back saying, "I feel so relaxed." I won't correct her and point out she means her *feet* feel relaxed. The pleasure felt by one part affects the whole. True family care begins as we recognize God intends for us to have a vital connection to one another.

The Bible simply assumes something unseen binds us together. The invisible bond of Christ tethers us to one another in the midst of life's experiences. Just as a rib injury can send waves of pain throughout the body, so too the suffering or joy of one member ought to radiate through the rest of the church. Elsewhere in the New Testament, this same mutual experience and care are commanded, "Rejoice with those who rejoice, weep with those who weep" (Romans 12:15).

Once again, you may need to think *natural family* for a moment. A natural family celebrates when a sibling has a baby or gets married. A natural family sheds tears with relatives who lose spouses or children to tragedy. Families celebrate new jobs and opportunities. They mourn loss and hardship. The rhythm of family life keeps time on the highs and lows of its members. The rhythm of the church should be no different. But the care of the local church is not about feeling alone.

As we've already seen, Biblical love compels us to action. We put the rubber of our brotherly love to the road of life in practical situations. Consider how the author of Hebrews exhorts the church to ongoing brotherly love, and then, in the next breath says, "Remember those who are in prison, as though in prison with them, and those who are mistreated, since you also are in the body" (Hebrews 13:3). The context of the book of Hebrews shows that the author did not urge the church to evangelistic ministries in prisons. He charged them to visit *one another* in prison. The original Hebrew-Christian readers of this letter suffered for their commitment to Christ. They had endured the hardship of public ridicule and shaming. Some had experienced the confiscation of property and imprisonment. The author calls upon the church to care for *these* men and women—those imprisoned for the sake of His Name. But don't miss the basis of the appeal to care for the imprisoned: "Remember those who are in prison, as though in prison with them, and those who are mistreated, *since you also are in the body*" (Hebrews 13:3, italics mine). Why would we act as if we're imprisoned? Because we're in the same body. You remember the principle, don't you? If one member suffers, all suffer together. If one member is imprisoned then it's as if the whole body has been thrown behind bars. And the outpouring of care that comes to the one member flows from the spiritual bond which unites them all.

As I've preached the Bible over the years, I've found that the accounts of the early church both move and confound contemporary Christians. There is beauty in what happened among those first disciples. They quickly devoted themselves to meeting together, receiving gospel teaching and celebrating their new fellowship (Acts 2:42). That's the part that moves people. Christians dream about what it might be like to be a part of such an intentional local church. But those first believers committed themselves to more than that.

The same converts who met and prayed together also sold their possessions and gave to brothers and sisters in need (Acts 2:45). Here's what confounds. Believers even sold property because of the same concern—others in the body had needs (Acts 4:32-37). Crazy? Not if you understand the principle beneath it. Men and women acted because they believed God had united them to one another as the body of Christ. They were members of one another and part of the family of God. Jesus called them to love. And love acts.

Throughout the rest of the New Testament, the church lives in accordance with this principle. The church in Jerusalem appointed deacons to meet an urgent need in distributing food to needy widows (Acts 6:1-6). Paul taught the church at Rome to contribute to the needs of the saints (Romans 12:13). The author of the book of Hebrews reminded his readers not to "neglect to do good and share what you have, for such sacrifices are pleasing to God" (Hebrews 13:16). Paul called the rich to share and thus live out Jesus' command to store up treasure in heaven (1 Timothy 6:17-19). He told Titus to teach his people to meet urgent needs (Titus 3:14), and the Ephesians to support widows whose natural families didn't provide for their needs (1 Timothy 5:3-16). Church members were part of a spiritual family who rallied to meet each other's needs.

All of this exemplifies the appeal to the Galatians to "bear one another's burdens, and so fulfill the law of Christ" (Galatians 6:2). The phrase "law of Christ" simply recasts Jesus' love command. Both practical and spiritual hardships burden the children of God. We labor under the strain of financial difficulty. We are pressed down by physical ailments. At times we're even worn thin by the scheduling demands of parenting, marriage, and career. We carry practical burdens and spiritual troubles. We struggle with daily temptations. We battle guilt, depression, and fear. We strive to press through the opposition of the world to know and follow Christ. Our burdens are real and our burdens are varied. But the calling to love beckons us—as members of the body—to throw ourselves under the weight of burden for others.

HOSPITALITY

If you want to get to know me, you should come to my house. When you walk in the front door, you'll see the bench I built in our entryway. You'll see how my wife and I remodeled our kitchen before we moved in. You'll see pictures of my kids and my garden out back. While you're in my home, you'll experience how I interact with my wife and kids. Being in my house means being in my life. This is what hospitality is all about. It begets familiarity and practical connection between believers. You might think of it as a shot in the arm of brotherly love.

It shouldn't surprise us then to find hospitality in some of the most pointed sections of Scripture addressing life in the local church. I've heard hospitality sometimes defined as *love for strangers*. Showing love to those we don't know could very well express Biblical hospitality. We will often have opportunities to welcome believers unknown to us (traveling gospel workers, missionaries on furlough, etc.). The context, however, of most New Testament commands to hospitality doesn't combat lack of acquaintance, but lack of love.

Paul tells the Romans, "Contribute to the needs of the saints and seek to show hospitality" (Romans 12:13). Those statements hang together. Contributing to the needs of the saints is coupled with hospitality because both show the family connection and care that should characterize the church. In fact, in Romans 12, family love over-arches all these commands. The paragraph calling us to hospitality begins with exhortations to genuine and brotherly love (vv. 9-10). Those exhortations flow from a prior discussion about the many members of the body being members "of one another" (v. 5). In other words, hospitality demonstrates our mutual love for one another within the church by opening ourselves to a relationship. Inviting others into our homes invites them into our lives.

Peter couples love and hospitality saying, "Above all, keep loving one another earnestly, since love covers a multitude of sins. Show hospitality to one another without grumbling" (1 Peter 4:8-9). Earnest love stretches itself. Much of the stretching comes as we open our home and life to other members of the church. For some, hospitality places an enormous hurdle in the path of love. Some naturally tend toward privacy and solitude. Some fear the awkwardness that can accompany new relationships. Others don't like the thought of having to cook for so many. Still others shy away from the potential of young children getting into—or even breaking—their belongings. But hospitality expresses love precisely because it overcomes these barriers to know and care for others. Hospitality chooses people over things and relationships over convenience.

Hospitality shows family love because—let's face it—that's what families do. Families get together. Families eat together. Families talk, laugh and share together. An open home means an open life.

AFFECTION

Loving one another goes far beyond mere emotion. Brotherly love acts in concrete demonstrations of family care. Feelings do not define Christian love. But neither is Christian love void of feelings.

Once again, we should think of the natural family. When my family gets together, the house is abuzz while people arrive. Their love for one another overflows through hugs, kisses, high fives and handshakes. Without these expressions, the joy of family commitment may wane. Action and feeling must be linked together in authentic family affection.

Imagine for a solid month I did everything in my power to serve my wife. I did laundry, detailed her car, cared for the kids so she could get some rest, and even bought her unexpected gifts. At the end of the month, she looks at me with eyes aglow and says, "I love you so much." As she speaks, she begins to invade my personal space. I quickly take a step back, nod my head and respond, "Thank you," before walking out of the room.

Here's the question: does she feel loved? If she questioned my love after my thankful but stoic nod, I could readily point to all the loving accomplishments of the past 30 days. But I would undermine my efforts if I didn't also show emotion. While the scriptures call us to actions which communicate the care and concern of a family, they also call us to show the affection of a family.

While not often highlighted because of the cultural differences, the New Testament authors speak of outward demonstrations of affection within the body of Christ. Paul calls upon the churches in Rome, Corinth and Thessalonica to greet one another with a "holy kiss" (Romans 16:16; 1 Corinthians 16:20; 2 Corinthians 13:12; 1 Thessalonians 5:26). Although the culture of the New Testament drove the particular form of these expressions,[10] they were not mere formalities. Holy kisses grew out of genuine love and spiritual kinship within the community of faith. In fact, Peter calls it the "kiss of love" (1 Peter 5:14).

Paul not only counseled this type of affection but also modeled it. Consider some of the things he said to local churches:

> "It is right for me to feel this way about you all, because
> I hold you in my heart... For God is my witness, how

I yearn for you all with the affection of Christ Jesus" (Philippians 1:7-8).

"So, being affectionately desirous of you, we were ready to share with you not only the gospel of God but also our own selves, because you had become very dear to us" (1 Thessalonians 2:8).

"For I wrote to you out of much affliction and anguish of heart and with many tears, not to cause you pain but to let you know the abundant love that I have for you" (2 Corinthians 2:4).

"...for I said before that you are in our hearts, to die together and to live together" (2 Corinthians 7:3b).

"and may the Lord make you increase and abound in love for one another and for all, as we do for you" (1 Thessalonians 3:12).

Desire. Affection. Love. Yearning. Holding in the heart. Those who view love as mere action don't speak this way. The apostle serves as a model in opening both his heart and life to brothers and sisters in the faith (1 Thessalonians 2:8).

Last year my elementary school daughter ran in the All-City cross-country meet. Onlookers lined the entire mile-long course for this final race of the year. I did what I could to prepare her. I talked to her about pacing. I made sure she hydrated throughout the day. I coached her about how fast to start and how to weave through the crowd of runners. All these tips helped, I think. But during the race, I noticed something remarkable. While leaning over the fencing on the side of the course, I spotted her coming my way. I began yelling, "Go, Amanda, you're doing great!!!" As soon as she heard my voice, her head snapped upright, and she started pumping her arms and running harder and faster. All of my support before the race was important, but it was my voice—my verbal affirmation—which spurred her on the most.

Maybe Paul knew affection and affirmation work this way in the spiritual realm. Perhaps he urged Christians in local churches to speak words of encouragement and greet one another in love for just this reason. Maybe this is why he called them to "outdo one another in showing honor" (Romans 12:10). All of our practical support and care for one another matters. But our voices and our hugs may spur our brothers and sisters on the most. We must not neglect the actions of love. But neither can we neglect the affection of love.

CONCLUSION

When you think of the church, you should think family. These people are deeply committed to you. They will be there for you when you need it. In exciting times or mundane moments, they will concern themselves with your good. They'll rejoice and weep by your side. They'll fill the gift table at your wedding and the waiting room during your surgery. They will share the joys and burdens of life. They'll open their homes and lives to you and put an arm around you and tell you you're loved. That's brotherly love. Love like family.

CHAPTER 3

LOVE DEFINED
(LOVE ON PURPOSE)

COLOSSIANS 1:28
Him we proclaim, warning everyone and
teaching everyone with all wisdom, that we
may present everyone mature in Christ.

A couple of years ago, I tried my hand at gardening. Although it never caught my interest before, something drew me to the idea of eating a salad from the backyard instead of the Walmart, so I tried to learn what I could. I researched online and discovered how seriously many people take their gardening. I read about people preparing their soil in the Fall for the following season. Gardeners posted articles about pH levels and soil testing. I watched videos of men burying fish in their gardens (either for the nutrients or as a pagan ritual—I'm still not sure which). I found information about weeding, spraying, watering and trellising. One woman shared that she kept a garden journal and visited her garden each day to record the progress of her plants. With a smirk I thought, *Who does this stuff?*

My first season was marginal, at best. I ran a small operation consisting of a few strawberry plants, peas, carrots and a lone tomato plant. I had glimmers of hope early on. But then the problems came. My strawberries rotted and attracted slugs. My peas produced for a week, but then fell over and got infected. My tomato plant produced one tomato which ended up splitting open before I could pick it (too much watering?). Oh, and my carrots apparently received less-than-optimal sunlight. When I pulled them, they resembled the smaller cousins of a bag of baby carrots. The smirk faded from my face as I thought back to my question, *Who does this stuff?* Now I knew: people who actually grow vegetables.

The Christian life is not unlike those garden plants. When men and women come to Christ, they enter a transformation of gradual renewal into the image of Christ. Their love for God increases. Their zeal to serve begins to grow. Their devotion to God's purposes deepens. Spiritual maturity comes bit by bit. Just like the plants in my garden, new believers take root with hope for a fruitful life in Christ. But just like the garden, growth doesn't happen automatically. God ordained the community of faith as the means of nurturing believers. Christian maturity, therefore, comes to fruition in and through the local church.

Understanding this principle should direct the life of the body of believers. We do not gather in aimless fellowship week after week. We labor so people might grow up into the head, Jesus Christ (Ephesians 4:15). We know what the garden should look like come harvest time. And because we do, we can begin to ask what will bring about the type of growth, maturity, and fruitfulness God intends. We don't have to hunt for the answer. God's word gives us practices designed to foster growth. Some practices fertilize and water young plants. Others serve as pest control or trellising. But they're all carried out with an eye toward believers growing in Christ, for His glory and their joy. So, how do we love on purpose?

INSTRUCT ONE ANOTHER

It's hard to overstate the importance of teaching. Jesus came as a teacher delivering God's truth. His words reoriented the disciples' thinking about their purpose, their sin and their need for forgiveness. He taught them about the kingdom of God. He taught in synagogues and the temple (Mark 1:21, 12:35). He taught on mountains and from boats (Matthew 5:2; Mark 4:1-2) He taught them from town to town and village to village (Matthew 9:35). He taught as One with authority, distinguishing Himself from the scribes (Matthew 7:29). Jesus didn't merely live and die for His people. He also imparted an interpretation of His life and death which would lead them to trust in Him. But the teaching mission didn't end with Him.

Jesus told His disciples that the Holy Spirit would come and teach them, guiding them into all truth (John 14:26, 16:13). Empowered by the Spirit, the apostles continued the teaching ministry. Following Christ's death and resurrection, they interpreted His sacrifice as the fulfillment of Old Testament themes and explained the good news to the masses. They did so through evangelistic proclamation and by instructing all who had responded to Christ by faith. In fact, the first 3,000 converts immediately committed themselves to learning (Acts 2:42). The apostles later placed such a value on teaching they decided to refrain from practical service ministries to give themselves wholly to the ministry of the word (Acts 6:2-4). Paul later told the Ephesian church to do the same, compensating gifted pastor-teachers who labored diligently to teach (1 Timothy 5:17). It's hard to overstate the importance of teaching.

Only by receiving sound teaching can new believers grow into a full knowledge of Christ. God uses His truth—taught by His people—as one of the primary means of spiritual nourishment. To revisit our gardening analogy, teaching is water. A gardener may do many things right. But if he doesn't water, nothing will grow. Christians may do many helpful and loving things for one another, but if the word of God does not regularly rain down on His people, no one will mature.

You may hear me tout the central place of teaching, and agree wholeheartedly. You've seen the damage of ministries devoid of sound teaching. You thank God for the faithful preaching of pastors who instruct and admonish the flock with God's word. But I want to push the discussion one step further. I'm not merely saying pastors ought to teach the flock. I'm saying the *flock* should teach the flock. We all have a calling from God to instruct one another. Sound teaching comes to God's people, but it must also come *through* God's people.

We often neglect to teach one another because we define teaching too narrowly. For many of you, the mere mention of teaching sends your mind back to high school speech class. You picture yourself being thrust before a lectern staring down a classroom full of judgmental peers just waiting to pounce on any mental misstep. You think about your voice seizing up, the queasy stomach, and that oft-quoted tip to picture people in their underwear (as if somehow that makes things *more* comfortable?). But formal instruction alone is not how we should think about our calling to instruct one another.

Teaching is often public and pastoral, but not always (1 Timothy 4:11-16; 2 Timothy 4:1-2). God has entrusted the teaching responsibility to all members of the local body. Paul told Titus to charge older women to fulfill their responsibility to teach younger women,

> Older women likewise are to be reverent in behavior, not slanderers or slaves to much wine. They are to teach what is good, and so train the young women to love their husbands and children, to be self-controlled, pure, working at home, kind, and submissive to their own husbands, that the word of God may not be reviled. (Titus 2:3-5)

Although their teaching ministry could've taken on a classroom-like structure, the context argues otherwise. Paul envisioned older women training the younger to *be* not merely to *know*. They aimed to instruct women for life and godliness. But the practical focus of their teaching didn't negate gospel content. All of their practical training grew out of Christ's redeeming work (Titus 2:11-14). Younger women learned from the older to treasure Christ and live in a way that adorned the gospel.

In Colossians Paul placed Christ front and center for all of life and ministry. He told the church they had been given fullness in Christ (Colossians 2:10), they should walk in and be rooted in Christ (2:6-7), and that they ought to hold fast to Christ (2:19). He also urged the whole church to, "Let the word of Christ dwell in you richly" (Colossians 3:16a). But he had a method in mind: "Let the word of Christ dwell in you richly, *teaching and admonishing one another* in all wisdom, singing psalms and hymns and spiritual songs, with thankfulness in your hearts to God" (Colossians 3:16, italics mine). The gospel dwells richly when men and women teach it. Paul didn't distinguish based on gender. He gave no age restrictions. Nor did he prescribe a format. He simply called members of the church to instruct one another. The gospel will permeate every corner of the church—bringing growth—as one believer teaches another.

Teaching brings maturity and serves as a sign of maturity. A congregation's teaching ability evidences its progress, or lack thereof. The author of Hebrews said, "For though by this time you ought to be teachers, you need someone to teach you again the basic principles of the oracles of God. You need milk, not solid food" (Hebrews 5:12). He didn't envision all Christians as pastors or public teachers. The principle lying beneath his criticism is the same we've seen in both Titus and Colossians. Local church members should have a vibrant ministry to one another teaching the truths of Christ. Each one should be equipped to pass on and apply basic Christian concepts to others.

I say *basic* because the author of Hebrews went on to mention things like repentance, faith, judgment and washings (Hebrews 6:1-2). Our ministry to one another is street-level, not graduate-level. We merely remind one another of the primary, foundational truths of the gospel. Knowing this will help us overcome a significant hurdle to fulfilling our teaching ministries.

Christians often refrain from teaching one another for fear they don't know enough. But the Bible doesn't require us to have expertise in theology before teaching one another. It simply requires genuine faith in Christ. Disciples teach other disciples. Do you remember the great commission passage from Matthew 28? Although often quoted with appeals to evangelism or missions, Christ's command contains another element, "Go therefore and make disciples of all nations, baptizing them in the name of the Father and of the Son and of the Holy Spirit, *teaching them to observe all that I have commanded you*" (Matthew 28:19-20a, italics mine). Making disciples means teaching disciples. Great commission work is teaching work.

God's truth through God's people matures God's church. Teaching is the spiritual water which grows the garden of God's kingdom. But all of our hands should pick up the hose.

ENCOURAGE AND EXHORT ONE ANOTHER

Not all Christians believe they need the local church. Many have fallen prey to the sirens beckoning them to isolation. Our technology adds to the spiritual solitude. You can go online to get theological teaching. With just a tap or two you can hear sermons from the best preachers in the world. You can worship the way you want, whether you've packed your playlist with classic hymns or Hillsong. And para-church organizations allow you to tether your tithe to whatever suits your fancy.

But do you notice anything missing? Do you see a gap anywhere? Can you put your finger on the problem? God designed for us to live our Christian lives with others. At your conversion God didn't merely save you out of something; He saved you into something—the church. God places us into a community of other believers who serve as instruments for our growth—and we for theirs. They help us live and remain faithful to the last day. Christians who detach themselves from the local church ignore God's intention and cut themselves off from the people who can spur them on to maturity. Local church members bear a responsibility to encourage one another in Christ.

The ministry of encouragement is broad and weaves itself into the diverse challenges we face. In my church people often speak of *coming alongside* one another. Coming alongside captures the essence of our responsibility to one another because it doesn't denote one specific action. It simply pictures a person there and ready to act in whatever way needed. We encourage based on what a given situation requires. With an eye toward helping a brother or sister mature and grow, the one who comes alongside communicates, "I'm here to help you follow and cling to Christ."

The New Testament describes the responsibility to come alongside with the Greek word *parakaleo*. Our English Bibles often render it "comfort." Jesus taught the crowds that the ones who mourn will be comforted (Matthew 5:4). He told a parable of a rich man and a servant named Lazarus who—while afflicted in life—received comfort in death (Luke 16:25). Paul praised God as the one who comforts us in our affliction (2 Corinthians 1:4). In each of these instances, *parakaleo* means relief for the sufferer. Those who mourn won't mourn. The afflicted find healing. Encouragement brings blessing and practical help. We should tune our hearts to the suffering and affliction of those in the body. And we ought to come alongside offering aid.

But *parakaleo* doesn't always mean comforting the afflicted. Often, our brothers and sisters don't have any particular suffering. But their lack of hardship doesn't remove our responsibility to come alongside. During normal times, *parakaleo* simply encourages others. In this case, we come alongside another Christian to inspire him or her to steadfast faith. Here, *parakaleo* doesn't cheer up; it cheers on. When Paul visited churches filled with new converts, he offered words of hope and strength,

> When they had preached the gospel to that city and had made many disciples, they returned to Lystra and to Iconium and to Antioch, strengthening the souls of the disciples, encouraging them to continue in the faith, and saying that through many tribulations we must enter the kingdom of God. (Acts 14:21-22)

A couple of years ago, I spent my summer training for a marathon. A friend of mine—a very experienced runner—agreed to run with me. Although we didn't train together, we stood shoulder to shoulder the morning of the race. Twenty miles into the course, my body hit something runners call "The Wall." The wall is an invisible point in the race where your body has depleted its stores of nutrition and hydration to such a degree that your legs can scarcely move. Needless to say, I struggled throughout the remainder of the race. But my faithful friend—running by my side—had somehow jumped over the proverbial wall. His nutrition and hydration were apparently excellent, so he had strength to encourage me along the way.

At one portion of the race, we crested a bridge near downtown. It provided a beautiful view of the park where the race would finish. My friend took the chance to point me forward. He reminded me of where we were and why I chose to run a marathon in the first place. This is the ministry of encouragement—*parakaleo*.

Encouragement is our responsibility and privilege within the body. Our corporate worship, in large part, serves as a setting to point one another forward. The author of Hebrews warned about neglecting corporate meetings of the church. "And let us consider how to stir up one another to love and good works, not neglecting to meet together, as is the habit of some, but encouraging one another, and all the more as you see the Day drawing near" (Hebrews 10:24-25). Don't miss the reason for his warning: our meetings provide an opportunity to spur on and point brothers and sisters forward in faithfulness in light of the coming Day of Christ.

We should come to worship gatherings not to take but to give. We must recognize that *parakaleo* flows both to us and from us when the church comes together. All around us sit less experienced runners—so to speak—worn by the demands of the day. Their spiritual energy and hydration stores may be depleted. But

God in His mercy has put them in our path so we might encourage them. German pastor and martyr Deitrich Bonhoeffer once wrote of the discouraged believer saying, "The Christ in his own heart is weaker than the Christ in the word of his brother."[11] The ministry of *parakaleo* calls us to come alongside and point weary ones toward the kingdom of God. We remind them of the goal and prize and of the One who called them to it.

Parakaleo comforts and encourages. But it also exhorts. Sometimes a person doesn't merely need comfort and relief. And encouragement to persevere isn't always enough. Every so often a person needs another believer to call him—with conviction and courage—to act. This is exhortation. In many instances where the New Testament uses the word *parakaleo*, the best English words for it are "appeal to," "plead with," "beg" or "urge." The context nearly demands a translation like this. If our ministry to one another is to be if faithful, it must plead, urge and appeal.

Earlier I described encouraging as cheering on. So let's go with the picture for a moment. Imagine a high school football player during a Friday night game. As he plays, he gives no notice to the cheerleaders on the sidelines chirping, "Go, fight, win!" But as the coaches stalk up and down the sidelines and one of them barks out "GO!" the young man snaps to attention and responds immediately. When the coach yells "GO!" a player knows he'd better do what he's told. The coach's words carry an urgency that the words of the cheer squad lack. Cheerleaders may encourage, but coaches exhort.

The Apostle Paul often spoke of warning or admonishing those around us. His words assume the same kind of urgency. When He issued his final instructions to the church at Rome, he said, "I appeal to you, brothers, to watch out for those who cause divisions and create obstacles contrary to the doctrine that you have been taught; avoid them" (Romans 16:17). Admonishment often comes into a context of potential threat. In Rome false teaching was a constant distraction. In Corinth division threatened to fracture the unity of the body. Paul admonished them saying "I *appeal* to you, brothers, by the name of our Lord Jesus Christ, that all of you agree, and that there be no divisions among you" (1 Corinthians 1:10, italics mine). Peter warned the church against the ever-present onslaught of the flesh saying, "Beloved, I *urge* you as sojourners and exiles to abstain from the passions of the flesh, which wage war against your soul" (1 Peter 2:11, italics mine). Urgent appeal—exhortation—therefore, ought not come with casual interest but blood-earnest care.

God uses admonishing one another as one of His tools to forge spiritual maturity. But just as we've seen with the ministry of instruction, the apostles and ministry "professionals" don't bear this responsibility alone. God intended exhortation to be the normal experience of *all* believers in the local church. It's one of the ways the gospel strengthens the body. "Let the word of Christ dwell in you richly, teaching and *admonishing one another* in all wisdom" (Colossians 3:16a, italics mine).

Parakaleo carries an element of urgency and warning. Spiritual threats require it. The author of Hebrews solemnly said,

> Take care, brothers, lest there be in any of you an evil, unbelieving heart, leading you to fall away from the living God. *But exhort one another every day,* as long as it is called "today," that none of you may be hardened by the deceitfulness of sin. For we have come to share in Christ, if indeed we hold our original confidence firm to the end. (Hebrews 3:12-14, italics mine)

The passage turns on the axis of exhortation because of what's at stake on either side. Unbelief grows in the soul. Christians can be led by unbelief to turn away from God. Sin deceives us, and with each lie our hearts become calloused with corruption. But exhortation answers all these threats.

God charges us to guard one another so no one walks away from Him. He calls us to help prevent evil and unbelieving hearts which would turn their backs on Christ. We must realize the world, the flesh and the devil assail our brothers and sisters with the false promises of sin. And we take to heart this eternal reality: only those who hold fast to Christ truly have any share with Christ. This is a call to mutual exhortation. And it's a call to *parakaleo*.

If you want to minister faithfully, you'll come alongside another member of the body. What you do when you get there will be determined by the need. One person may need you to offer the relief of comfort and care. Another may crave a word of strengthening as you remind them of the great hope of the gospel. Still others require the urgent plea to faithfulness in the face of ever-threatening temptation. As Paul told the church at Thessalonica, "And we urge you, brothers, admonish the idle, encourage the fainthearted, help the weak, be patient with them all" (1 Thessalonians 5:14).

If we use the garden analogy again, *parakaleo* represents the trellising. We see a vine fallen away from the gospel stake. In order for it to thrive, it must be securely fastened to Christ. With our words and our presence, we restore others to a position of trust and dependence to help them grow. God entrusts us with a ministry of comfort, encouragement, and exhortation in Christ. But we must remember it's never just a ministry to one another *in* Christ; it's always a ministry that brings us closer *to* Christ.

SERVE ONE ANOTHER

The night of Jesus' betrayal He performed an act meant to arrest attention and inspire action. Jesus Christ—the incarnate Son of God (Matthew 1:23)—got up from the table to wash the feet of His disciples. They neither requested nor expected the Lord to serve them this way. Rabbis didn't wash feet. Only menial servants undertook such a task.[12] But the Lord Jesus—towel wrapped around Him—stooped to serve.

Perhaps it shouldn't surprise us that Jesus acted this way. His entire mission, after all, displayed humility and service. His obscure birth bore witness to the type of life He would lead. Jesus became a man to serve man. Paul spoke of the humility of Christ saying, "Who, though he was in the form of God, did not count equality with God a thing to be grasped, but emptied himself, by taking the form of a servant, being born in the likeness of men" (Philippians 2:6-7). The very humanity of Christ signaled His care and desire to serve. And He fulfilled that desire throughout His earthly ministry. While healing, casting out demons and speaking words of hope to the downtrodden, this Son-of-God-in-the-flesh had His eyes on one great final act of service, "For even the Son of Man came not to be served but to serve, and to give his life as a ransom for many" (Mark 10:45).

The picture of our towel-draped Lord scraping the midday dirt from His disciples' toes wasn't intended to say something merely about His mission. He intended His humility to become the paradigm of service for *ours*. "You call me Teacher and Lord, and you are right, for so I am. If I then, your Lord and Teacher, have washed your feet, you also ought to wash one another's feet. For I have given you an example, that you also should do just as I have done to you" (John 13:13-15).

Paul told the Galatians, "For you were called to freedom, brothers. Only do not use your freedom as an opportunity for the flesh, but through love serve one another" (Galatians 5:13). Love comes through service. Service expresses our love. Considering again the example of a husband who served his wife but avoided any outward expression of love, I want you to picture the opposite. A husband gushes with loving words to his wife, making sure she daily knows his boyish adoration. But each day, she needs his help. They have kids to care for, a yard to mow, and home repairs to make. He does nothing. But each time he refuses to serve his wife, he takes her in his arms to say, "But I want you to know how much I love you!" How long would it take before those words fell flat? Service must match our words of love, or else our words of love are just empty sentimentality. The Apostle John said,

> By this we know love, that he laid down his life for us, and we ought to lay down our lives for the brothers. But if anyone has the world's goods and sees his brother in need, yet closes his heart against him, how does God's love abide in him? Little children, *let us not love in word or talk but in deed and in truth.* (1 John 3:16-18, italics mine)

But how should we serve one another? Peter succinctly answered, "As each has received a gift, use it to serve one another, as good stewards of God's varied grace" (1 Peter 4:10). Those redeemed by Christ are given the capacity to bless and build up His church. The New Testament doesn't lead us to view gifts as simple talents or abilities, but rather deposits of empowering grace in the lives of His children. Consider Paul's reference to grace in 1 Corinthians 15, "But by the grace of God I am what I am, and his grace toward me was not in vain. On the contrary, I worked harder than any of them, though it was not I, but the grace of God that is with me" (v. 10). God gave vital energy to Paul's service in the gospel. Paul worked and labored, but in the last estimation he knew God's grace and power worked through him. Spiritual gifts work just this way. God's power flows through his people.

God empowers all Christians for service, but not in the same way. Picture God's enabling grace as breath blowing into our souls. When His breath of grace comes through each of us, it comes as through a musical instrument. Different wind instruments may make different sounds, but all of them owe their music to the breath blowing through them. So it is with the empowering grace of God. According to His will, the way His grace moves each believer differs from one to the next. But all are united by this simple fact: God's grace empowers God's people. Listen to how Peter considers different categories of gifts: "Whoever speaks, as one who speaks oracles of God; whoever serves, as one who serves by the strength that God supplies—in order that in everything God may be glorified through Jesus Christ. To Him belong glory and dominion forever and ever. Amen" (1 Peter 4:11). Why does God get the glory? Because God gave the power.

Realizing God graciously empowers us should motivate our hearts to exercise our gifts unto His glory. We do this by serving one another. In fact, the winds of God's grace blow with this in mind. The apostle Paul wrote to the church at Corinth saying, "To each is given the manifestation of the Spirit for the common good" (1 Corinthians 12:7). We seek the common good—as 1 Corinthians 12-14 makes clear—as we build up the saints. Each church member should exercise his Spirit-given, God-empowered capacity to serve, to encourage the body of Christ to grow in love for Him.

One Christmas morning my wife had me close my eyes while she carried my present from the garage. I opened my eyes to see a new snow shovel—complete with red and white bow. Because I had been asking for one, the shovel brought me joy. But even while it was *for* me, I knew it had a purpose *beyond* me. The shovel came with an expectation—I should use it for the good of our household. My family would reap the benefit of my gift, even as it brought me joy to use.

Both Romans and 1 Corinthians contain lists of gifts God gives to His children. From teaching to administration, prophecy to giving, God has showered His church with grace. But just like my snow shovel, these gifts carry an implicit expectation: the gift has a purpose beyond you. God's power working through us brings great joy, but it also comes with the expectation we'll use it for the good of our spiritual household. Or in the words of Paul, "So with yourselves, since you are eager for manifestations of the Spirit, strive to excel in building up the church" (1 Corinthians 14:12).

PRAY FOR ONE ANOTHER

Since we've been focusing a good bit of attention on gardening images through this chapter, I want to draw your attention to one final truth from the world of agriculture. Farmers used to pray for rain. For most of human history, extensive farming operations couldn't depend upon mechanical equipment for irrigating crops. Men depended upon the movement of the skies. Most understood God (or a god, in pagan cultures) to be responsible for the waters of life and growth. In spite of all our efforts and labors, we can't make anything grow.

It's the same for the church. We can labor, serve, speak and use our gifts. But we can't make people grow. In His parables of the growing kingdom, Jesus highlights this point, "And he said, 'The kingdom of God is as if a man should scatter seed on the ground. He sleeps and rises night and day, and the seed sprouts and grows; he knows not how'" (Mark 4:26-27). We do not bring the kingdom; God does. Paul highlighted the same idea as he contrasted our labors with God's work in His people. "I planted, Apollos watered, but God gave the growth. So neither he who plants nor he who waters is anything, but only God who gives the growth" (1 Corinthians 3:6-7). Paul labored hard. Apollos taught the church. But when the crops came, neither stood back and said, "Look what I've done!" It was beyond them, and they knew it. Only through God's gracious power can growth and health come to the people of God. When Paul spoke to the Colossians about holding fast to Christ the Head, he told them that "the whole body, nourished and knit together through its joints and ligaments, grows with a growth that is from God" (Colossians 2:19).

What should the church do in light of this principle? Pray. Don't let that surprise you. God has always called His children to depend on Him. Christ taught His disciples to persist in prayer (Luke 11:8-9). He showed them how continuing in prayer expressed faith (Luke 18:1-8). When the first preaching of the gospel birthed the Jerusalem church, the first 3,000 converts devoted themselves to prayer (Acts 2:42). First-century churches were taught to depend on God through prayer. "Continue steadfastly in prayer, being watchful in it with thanksgiving" (Colossians 4:2). "Rejoice in hope, be patient in tribulation, be constant in prayer" (Romans 12:12); "Pray without ceasing" (1 Thessalonians 5:17). This attitude of constant prayer creates a church able to mature and serve one another in love.

The church should pray because of our responsibility for love and mutual edification. We aim to love and serve one another so the body of Christ matures (Ephesians 4:13). So, what does a praying church look like when it's seeking the growth of its members? It looks like a people laboring in prayer for one another. In fact, when we consider the context of the appeals to faithful prayer in the New Testament, we begin to hear echoes of the life of the body in the church's prayers.

When Paul charged the church to pray steadfastly (Colossians 4:2), he immediately asked them to pray for him. His ministry efforts—even his boldness proclaiming the gospel—needed the prayers of the saints. When he encouraged the Roman church to be constant in prayer, he did so in a section dominated by others-directed thinking. Romans 12:9 urges the church to "Let love be genuine." Like a banner over the rest of the passage, the calling to love helps define our constancy in prayer.[13] In other words, we do not pray persistently for our own lives and concerns alone. Instead, emblazoned on our hearts are the spiritual concerns of our brothers and sisters.

God has given the spiritually embattled church the resources to stand firm in Christ against the wiles of the devil. We take God's armor to prepare for the enemy's schemes. We even wield the sword of the Spirit. In addition to these weapons, we pray "at all times in the Spirit, with all prayer and supplication. To that end keep alert with all perseverance, making supplication for all the saints" (Ephesians 6:18). Our perseverance in prayer has not only our spiritual survival in mind but that of the whole church. We pray *all* kinds of prayers for *all* the saints. We ask for evangelistic boldness and opportunity (Colossians 4:3-4). We pray for those caught in sin (1 John 5:16). We pray for those who have confessed their sin and need the healing grace of God (James 5:16). We pray for satisfaction in Christ's love (Ephesians 3:15-19), lives worthy of the gospel (Colossians 1:10), and enlightened hearts to know the power of God (Ephesians 1:16-19). The fight to stand firm in Christ is a fight of prayer. And it's a corporate fight.

Each time I teach our church's membership class, I tell potential members they have a responsibility to pray for one another. I say that even if they don't know everyone, they can still hold other members in earnest prayer. I show them my paper directory with pictures of hundreds of members—notes scribbled in the margins—and tell them aside from their Bible, their member directory is the most important book they have for faithful membership in our church. Why? Because we aim to see men and women built up in Christ, standing firm in the faith. Because we work for growth, serving and encouraging one another in love. And none of these things succeeds apart from God's blessing.

Oh, that we might come into the presence of God with persistent, devoted purpose for ALL the saints. That we might all reflect the life of Epaphras, that great servant of God, who set an example of "struggling on your behalf in his prayers, that you may stand mature and fully assured in all the will of God" (Colossians 4:12). Our efforts will never bring the church to maturity. But God's abundant grace can. So we pray for rain on behalf of all of the saints.

CHAPTER 4

LOVE DEFINED (LOVE THROUGH CONFLICT)

PSALM 133
A Song of Ascents. Of David.
Behold, how good and pleasant it is
when brothers dwell in unity!
It is like the precious oil on the head,
running down on the beard, on the beard of Aaron,
running down on the collar of his robes!
It is like the dew of Hermon,
which falls on the mountains of Zion!
For there the Lord has commanded the blessing,
life forevermore.

Situated among the great "psalms of ascent," Psalm 133 both celebrates and pictures the blessing of unity among God's people. The psalmist recalls the oil of anointing which set the priests apart from other Israelites. The oil marked them off as distinct. Devoted to God, these priests served and represented Him to the people. The psalmist also mentioned the dew of Hermon signifying the practical provision of God. Here, the land drank in His blessing, which meant abundance for His people.

Now, if we combine those two images, we begin to see just what's at stake in the unity of the church. Unity sets God's people apart and marks them off as devoted to Him. Our life, bound up and knit together in heart, mind and spirit marks off the church as distinct—and distinctly God's. Unity also pours forth blessing. In a way similar to the dew falling on the mountains, the harmony and love that exist among the children of God brings spiritual encouragement. God pours His grace into our lives through His people.

The celebration of unity among God's people reverberates through the New Testament as well. Although it comes to us in different language, the heart is the same. When God's people live in joyful unity it gives credence to the gospel that created it.

Consider Jesus' words to His disciples: "Salt is good, but if the salt has lost its saltiness, how will you make it salty again? Have salt in yourselves, and be at peace with one another" (Mark 9:50). The salt metaphor doesn't envision each Christian individually. Instead, Jesus called His people to be salt *as a people*. For this reason, when He repeated the salt image, He added to it, "Have salt in yourselves, and be at peace with one another." We cannot disconnect saltiness from peace. The one defines the other.[14] Our peaceful relationships as disciples constitute our saltiness in the world.

All through the New Testament the local church is assumed as the primary context in which the disciples of Christ "live at peace" with one another. Listen to some of the repeated encouragement Paul gives to local churches: "Finally, brothers, rejoice. Aim for restoration, comfort one another, agree with one another, live in peace; and the God of love and peace will be with you" (2 Corinthians 13:11). "And let the peace of Christ rule in your hearts, to which indeed you were called in one body. And be thankful. (Colossians 3:15). "Be at peace among yourselves" (1 Thessalonians 5:13b). In these texts we can feel the undercurrent of Psalm 133. The body of Christ should display loving community distinct from anything the world has to offer. This is what it means to be "salt of the earth" kind of people.

But Paul also speaks of the life of the body with the language of harmony. "Live in harmony with one another. Do not be haughty, but associate with the lowly. Never be wise in your own sight" (Romans 12:16). For those who know music, the image may have more of an effect. Harmony occurs when someone coordinates many distinct parts into one song. The parts make something beautiful because of how they come together.

Harmony in the church is no different. Something uniquely glorifying to God occurs when many disciples, with distinct backgrounds, incomes, families, heritage, etc., come together in Christ. When the church lives in mutual care and love, it becomes a song the world loves to hear. For this reason, Paul prays for the church in these terms: "May the God of endurance and encouragement grant you to live in such harmony with one another, in accord with Christ Jesus, that together you may with one voice glorify the God and Father of our Lord Jesus Christ" (Romans 15:5-6).

Peace. Harmony. And of course, unity. Jesus prayed for unity as He interceded on behalf of His disciples (John 17:21-23). He did so because Christian unity would validate the gospel to the watching world. Therefore, while unity is a good and pleasant gift, it's also a command to faithful disciples. Paul began his first letter to the Corinthians saying, "I appeal to you, brothers, by the name of our Lord Jesus Christ, that all of you agree, and that there be no divisions among you, but that you be united in the same mind and the same judgment" (1 Corinthians 1:10). Many forms of disunity had already beset the Corinthian church. Factionalism (1:12), arrogance (4:6), lawsuits (6:1), and even socio-economic distinctions during celebration of the Lord's table (11:22) plagued them. The answer? Unity.

The church can be united because it is fastened together by an unbreakable gospel bond. Each believer united to Christ at conversion is thereby joined to His people. Or, as Paul would later say,

> I therefore, a prisoner for the Lord, urge you to walk in a manner worthy of the calling to which you have been called, with all humility and gentleness, with patience, bearing with one another in love, eager to maintain the unity of the Spirit in the bond of peace. There is one body and one Spirit—just as you were called to the one hope that belongs to your call— one Lord, one faith, one baptism, one God and Father of all, who is over all and through all and in all. (Ephesians 4:1-6)

Our theological unity must drive us to pursue practical unity. We realize there is One God and One Spirit blowing in the lives of all of His people. We pursue unity and maintain peace because we truly are unified in the Son of God who gave eternal peace.

At this point, some of you might be thinking, "I thought this chapter had to do with conflict?" My goal in this chapter is to show how to love one another amid sin and failure. But that goal can only be seen against the backdrop of unity God intends for His church. Only when we understand and yearn for the unity, harmony, and peace which ought to characterize the church, are we ready to combat what threatens it.

A few years ago, my young daughters ran in from the backyard to tell me they felt something "pokey" in the grass. When I went to inspect, I noticed sharp—yes, "pokey"—weeds had overtaken a whole section of our yard. After some failed attempts to spray them, I decided to up the ante. Over the next hour and a half, I dug up each weed.

Now, you might think that's a bit excessive. But that's just it. I couldn't care less about going after weeds. So why did I do it? Those weeds threatened what my yard was supposed to be. In my backyard, my kids should be able to run barefoot, kick balls and do cart-wheels to their heart's content. The weeds only concerned me because they began to destroy all of that.

We must always keep in view that when we love one another through conflict, we do so not because we have some attraction to confrontation. Instead, we press through because we've seen the majesty of what the unified church was designed by God to be.

So, God calls us to peace, unity and harmony within the church. But just how should we maintain, protect and restore these precious blessings?

DON'T BE MEAN TO ONE ANOTHER

At our church we teach a principle called, "Don't be mean." You might first think it's a portion of the children's curriculum. Perhaps, an orientation to kindergarten Sunday school? Nope. "Don't be Mean" is a section of our membership class. We teach 25 to 85-year-olds alike that part of Christ's calling for them is not to be mean to each other. A bit tongue-in-cheek? Maybe. But with that humor we mean to sum up a broad swath of the New Testament's teaching for the body of Christ.

The New Testament authors often include vice lists in their letters. These lists don't merely condemn those outside the church, but rather they admonish those within it. Saved sinners, after all, make up the membership rolls of any local congregation. And although Christ justifies us in a moment, His Spirit makes us holy only over time. Translation: we still sin. Specifically, we even sin against one another. The apostles warned churches about sins which appealed to their old nature and would threaten their life of unity and peace.

For example, Paul appealed to the Ephesians to let go of bitterness, wrath, anger, clamor and slander (Ephesians 4:31). Or... don't be mean. He told the Colossians to put away anger, wrath, malice, slander, obscene talk and lies (Colossians 3:7-9). Or... don't be mean. James spoke of quarrels, selfish motives and grumbling against one another (James 4:1-11, 5:9). Or... don't be mean. And Peter called the church to put away malice, deceit, hypocrisy, envy, and slander (1 Peter 2:1). How should we sum all of this up? Hmm? How about: "Don't be mean?"

But think carefully about what we ought to remove. The sins Paul, Peter and James mention affect others. They erode the good foundation of mutual love and care upon which unity and peace are built. God doesn't mean to give a list of "no-nos" for His church to nitpick. The prohibitions exist because of what's on the line. Those sins vandalize and jeopardize something profoundly glorious—the life of love within God's church.

We protect the unity of the church when we avoid vices like these. But we will never do it perfectly, so what do we do when sin enters the camp?

BEAR WITH ONE ANOTHER

The first line of defense against the destruction of the body of Christ is merely bearing with one another. Paul instructs the Colossians: "Put on then, as God's chosen ones, holy and beloved, compassionate hearts, kindness, humility, meekness, and patience, *bearing with one another* and, if one has a complaint against another, forgiving each other; as the Lord has forgiven you, so you also must forgive" (Colossians 3:12-13, italics mine). Let's recast that in more common terms. Bearing with one another means we simply put up with one another. Some of you likely just had the air taken out of your sails. After all of these glorious and inspiring Biblical pictures of love in the local church, I'm simply telling you to put up with each other? Yes. I'm saying putting up with others in the body expresses your love for them.

Marriage provides a great example of bearing with another person. In marriage, two people covenant together for life. They share the joys of life and press through the everyday rubs of shared space and responsibility. Any marriage has both small sins and significant failures. But we don't confront them all the same way. A woman doesn't sit her husband down for a serious talk every time he tromps through the house with wet boots. She doesn't ask to see a counselor when he leaves shaving stubble in the bathroom sink. What does she do? She puts up with it. She puts up with him. Likewise, a man doesn't confront his wife each time she forgets to mail a check or pick up the kids from practice. He bears with her. Even when a spouse sins against us, we can bear with another fallen saint. These repeated decisions to put up with something are actually simple acts of love.

Consider Peter's words, drawn from the book of Proverbs: "Above all, keep loving one another earnestly, since *love covers a multitude of sins*" (1 Peter 4:8, italics mine). True, sometimes love means speaking the truth and confronting sin. We'll get to that. But often, love means looking at the sins of another person and going to get a rug. We bring it back and cover their sins so they lie out of our emotional sight. We move on in the joy of relationship because, in love, we're willing to put up with it. Paul includes in his description of love, "Love bears all things, believes all things, hopes all things, endures all things" (1 Corinthians 13:7). Marriages can crumble under the weight of offenses and failures. The church ceases to shine when she does not cover over imperfections and sins. So put up with each other—in love.

GO TO ONE ANOTHER

At times bearing with one another doesn't apply. In cases of more serious sin or developing patterns, we have a responsibility to confront those we love. We should go with grace, humility, and the goal of promoting repentance. But we must go nonetheless.

In our culture confronting a brother or sister may prove the most challenging way to express Christian love. We live in a time when "to each his own" rules the day. Tolerance and approval of any preference or life choice define the new morality. Our culture loves to view Jesus as an old pull-string toy. Each time you go to Him, you pull the string and hear, "Judge not, lest ye be judged." But this not only views Christ and His teaching falsely, it also warps our view of how to act within the church.

Ironically, the passage our culture uses to argue against judgment assumes we *will* lovingly confront others. In the Sermon on the Mount, Jesus didn't prohibit judgment of every kind. He forbade judgment of a particular kind. He taught His disciples to avoid judgment without introspection and humility. A person with hypocritical judgment looks at another person with an eye of critique but can't see anything in himself. Jesus follows the famous "judge not" passage with teaching about the plank and speck. "Why do you see the speck that is in your brother's eye, but do not notice the log that is in your own eye?" (Matthew 7:3). If we obey Jesus' words, we should have a healthy level of self-awareness about our sin. And yet the purpose of the log/speck metaphor remains: "You hypocrite, first take the log out of your own eye, and then you will see clearly to take the speck out of your brother's eye" (Matthew 7:5). What's the point of dealing with my log? My brother's speck. I'm to humbly evaluate myself so I can assess and confront my brother with integrity.

The New Testament assumes loving confrontation will happen among God's people. Jesus taught His disciples to watch over one another saying, "Pay attention to yourselves! If your brother sins, rebuke him, and if he repents, forgive him" (Luke 17:3). We pay attention so we can rebuke when necessary. Jesus called His disciples to pursue those entangled in sin: "If your brother sins against you, go and tell him his fault, between you and him alone. If he listens to you, you have gained your brother" (Matthew 18:15). In these passages repentance—turning from sin—results when a Christian first goes to the one in sin, and second tells him his fault. Just as God uses the body of Christ to bring His blessing, grace, and love, so too, He uses the church to bring about repentance and restoration.

James closed his letter by saying, "My brothers, if anyone among you wanders from the truth and someone brings him back, let him know that whoever brings back a sinner from his wandering will save his soul from death and will cover a multitude of sins" (James 5:19-20). Paul pleads with the Galatian church: "Brothers, if anyone is caught in any transgression, you who are spiritual should restore him in a spirit of gentleness. Keep watch on yourself, lest you too be tempted" (Galatians 6:1).

He calls us to go. He calls us to speak. He calls us to do both with a heart yearning to see a brother repentant and restored. But we must go humbly and gently. Jesus' plank and speck metaphor constrains us to humble introspection when confronting a brother or sister. How can I look down my nose at the sin of another when I've just come from confessing my own before God? We also go in a spirit of gentleness. Gentleness carries the strength to weather a brother's potentially harsh initial response. We remain calm and steadfast in purpose, exhibiting the humility of Christ as we call him back to the narrow road.

But this humble, self-reflective, gentle manner of confronting a brother also serves him. Harsh condemnation often elicits strong self-justification (Proverbs 15:1). Humble rebukes—given in a Spirit of gentleness—may foster a softer response and readiness to hear God's word.

We know we should go to a brother in sin. We know how to go. And yet we must never forget why we go. We speak the truth in love and we love most deeply by caring for another's soul. Bonhoeffer wrote, "Nothing can be crueler than the tenderness that consigns another to his sin. Nothing can be more compassionate than the severe rebuke that calls a brother back from the path of sin."[15] When we go to a brother, we don't go because we're disgusted by their sins, nor do we go to flaunt our righteousness by comparison. We go because apostasy threatens. A person turned away from God in sin is turned away from God. He travels down a road which ends in destruction. The author of Hebrews spoke of sin's blinding effect as well as our responsibility to one another: "Take care, brothers, lest there be in any of you an evil, unbelieving heart, leading you to fall away from the living God. But exhort one another every day, as long as it is called "today," that none of you may be hardened by the deceitfulness of sin" (Hebrews 3:12-13).

What's at stake in the humble, faithful work of confronting our brothers and sisters? Eternity. Only those who hold fast to Christ have a share in Him (Hebrews 3:14). Going to one another with love, humility and purpose helps weak hands hold on to Christ for the long haul. Sin deceives and leads us to wander. But the church speaks the truth, and in love, turns sinners from error to eternity.

FORGIVE ONE ANOTHER

Growing up I listened weekly to a building full of people dutifully recite the Lord's prayer. Years later—after being converted—I saw the Lord's prayer with new eyes. I no longer counted it a ritual but viewed it as important teaching for my life of discipleship. In this prayer, Jesus guided me to revere God's name and yearn for His honor. He beckoned me to bow my heart to God's kingdom instead of laboring to establish my own. He taught me to rely daily on God's provision and seek His will in all things. And Jesus expected me to forgive.

Nestled between daily bread and deliverance from evil lies an implicit call, "and forgive us our debts, as we also have forgiven our debtors" (Matthew 6:12). God has woven forgiveness into our daily devotion. Christians forgive. And for a good reason.

We forgive because God forgave us. From beginning to end, the message of Christ promises forgiveness. Jesus called the gospel a message of "repentance and the forgiveness of sins" (Luke 24:47). When Christians come together to celebrate the Lord's table, they remember Christ and the forgiveness He secured in reciting, "For this is my blood of the covenant, which is poured out for many for the forgiveness of sins" (Matthew 26:28). Forgiveness is one of the crowning jewels of God's saving grace.

But the jewel of forgiveness doesn't merely adorn salvation. God forgave expecting us to do the same. After instructing His disciples how to *confront* sin, Jesus immediately addressed how to *forgive* sin. The question came from Peter who wondered how much forgiveness God required. In response, Jesus told a humbling parable of a king and a servant. The servant owed an unimaginable sum, but the king canceled his debt. The servant, however, did not reproduce the vast forgiveness of the king. He demanded a fellow servant repay him a small debt—a pittance when compared with the debt the king had canceled. The servant demonstrated that the king's mercy didn't produce even the slightest impulse to forgive (Matthew 18:21-35).

The parable rattles us because the appropriate action for the servant is so apparent: forgive. Our hearts rage against the idea of one receiving such kindness, then withholding mercy from others. But if our hearts rage against this idea in a parable, then they should also cry out for forgiveness in our own lives. Our debt of sin was unimaginable. We had rebelled against the almighty God of creation, yet He released us. Christ paid the debt and we walked free. So how can we fail to forgive others? Others' sin against us is like the pittance owed to the wicked servant. It cannot compare with the mountain of our own sin that our God cast into the heart of the sea (Micah 7:19). And if He has cast ours away, shouldn't we cast theirs?

A healthy, thriving church overflows with forgiveness. "Be kind to one another, tenderhearted, forgiving one another, as God in Christ forgave you" (Ephesians 4:32); "bearing with one another and, if one has a complaint against another, forgiving each other; as the Lord has forgiven you, so you also must forgive" (Colossians 3:13). Just as in the parable, the "ought" of forgiveness comes as we glance back at the cross. We must forgive because we've been forgiven. But we must also see that forgiveness expresses Christ-centered love.

Forgiveness—at its most basic—lets go of something.[16] When we forgive, we let offenses go. We release the feelings of ill-will and hostility which usually go with conflict. True forgiveness doesn't demand retribution or payback. It lets go. If we hope to love through conflict, we must see forgiveness as the last frontier. When we've done all we can do, the only real hope for peace rides on one forgiven sinner willing to forgive another.

Years ago, I took a seminary class dealing with practical, pastoral theology. One of the sections covered forgiveness. After much discussion—and many attempts to define it—our professor summed up forgiveness this way: "Forgiveness... it's when I take my hands off of your neck".

Offenses will come. Our brothers and sisters will fail us, hurt us and even sin against us. But as the redeemed of God, we bow our knees each day before the Father of grace. We remember how He's released us. And we pray for strength to do the same for others. Because we aim for health and unity within the body, we loosen our spiritual hands and release those who've sinned against us. When we loosen the grip of condemnation, we do so to embrace them once more in a spirit of love.

BE RECONCILED TO ONE ANOTHER

Forgiveness is not the goal. Peace, unity, and harmony are. Reconciliation restores formerly hostile parties to joyful relationship.[17]

Reconciliation should characterize the church because Christ's cross purchased it as one of the central blessings of salvation. At one time we were alienated from God and hostile to Him (Romans 5:10, 8:7; Colossians 1:21). We fought against Him, and He held wrath for us. But when Christ died upon the tree, our sins of hostility and rebellion died with Him. So did God's burning anger. Christ bore our curse (Galatians 3:13) and restored us to fellowship with Almighty God (1 Peter 3:18). He reconciled us by the blood of His cross (Colossians 1:22). In fact, reconciliation is so central to the gospel that Paul even called our mission to proclaim it a "ministry of reconciliation" (2 Corinthians 5:18).

The gospel reconciles us to God, but it also reconciles us to one another. In Ephesians Paul laid these side by side, showing that the cross of Christ accomplishes reconciliation in both directions: "For he himself is our peace, who has made us both one and has broken down in his flesh the dividing wall of hostility by abolishing the law of commandments expressed in ordinances, that he might create in himself one new man in place of the two, so making peace, and might reconcile us both to God in one body through the cross, thereby killing the hostility" (Ephesians 2:14-16).

Earlier in Ephesians Paul described Jews and Gentiles (non-Jews) as hostile and divided. Jews had the promises of God, the covenants of the Old Testament, and citizenship in the kingdom of God. Gentiles were excluded from all of these. But God intervened through the cross of Christ to reconcile both groups to Himself. A Jew doesn't inherit salvation through his lineage but through Christ. The same holds true for a Gentile. Only the work of Christ can restore a sinner to a relationship with God. But this restoring work also affects human relationships. The cross of Christ dismantles the wall of separation between sinners and God, and between one another.

We should reconcile with one another not only because God has reconciled us, but also because He desires healthy churches to live in unity. Unity can't survive while relational strains persist. Paul charged the Corinthian church—one plagued by strife and division—to pursue this ideal: "Finally, brothers, rejoice. Aim for restoration, comfort one another, agree with one another, live in peace; and the God of love and peace will be with you" (2 Corinthians 13:11). Restoration, peace and renewed unity aren't optional for the people of God. They're blood-bought necessities. And unless we reconcile, we cannot pursue the glory of God together. Jesus instructed His disciples, "So if you are offering your gift at the altar and there remember that your brother has something against you, leave your gift there before the altar and go. First be reconciled to your brother, and then come and offer your gift" (Matthew 5:23-24). God has woven healthy relationships into the meaning of discipleship. We can't follow Him, obey Him or worship Him faithfully without working toward healthy relationships.

A few years ago I began rock climbing with a friend. We learned all we could about the sport and how to safely enjoy it. One of the critical safety concepts in climbing is redundancy. Climbers set up redundant systems by putting backups in place. For instance, at the top of the rock two sets of straps and carabiners hold the rope. If one system fails, the other will save your life.

As I consider the last two sections, it seems that God has built redundancy into the life of the church. If someone has sinned against me, I'm called to go to him. I speak the truth in love, hoping for repentance and restoration. But from the other end, if I know anyone has something against me, I should go to him. Why? To reconcile. So whether I'm the offender or the offended, I'm commanded go to my brother hoping to restore the unity we ought to have. Redundancy. If one system fails, another will save the life of the church.

CONCLUSION

God counts our unity, peace, and harmony too precious to be jeopardized by works of sinful flesh. He calls us away from community destroying sins. He asks us to put to death anything that would dismantle our love. He calls us to bear with the failings and imperfections of brothers and sisters, and to do the hard, humbling work of loving confrontation. He commands us to forgive freely when we've won a brother or sister to the path of life. God wants a community of restored relationships which continually bears witness to His work and character as the reconciling God.

CHAPTER 5

LOVE EMPOWERED

1 JOHN 4:7

Beloved, let us love one another, for love is from God, and
whoever loves has been born of God and knows God.

Every summer my wife and I block off time to take our kids camping. For you backpackers, calling it camping may mislead. At this stage in life, we camp with a hard-shell trailer dragged behind a half ton Chevy. We rough it with dry beds, modest lights, a sink and yes, even a refrigerator. Our trailer provides many comforts when we brave the campground. But we also pack a little extra insurance: the generator. Anytime I need to power up the trailer battery—or microwave some popcorn—I just pull the rope and listen to the hum of 1800 watts of comfort. The generator provides all the power we need.

If you ask me why the generator works, I could offer many answers. I might tell you it works because I pull the rope and start the engine. Or, I could describe how the motor turns the shaft rotating the coil magnets. And while not untrue, those answers miss something more fundamental. A generator only works if you put gas in it. Power goes out because gas goes in. A generator produces power when fueled to do so.

The scriptures paint an impressive portrait of the church's life. As a family the church offers mutual care and concern to all its members. They bear one another's burdens and work through conflict. They aim to stimulate growth in each member of the body. But this impressive portrait is also costly. Biblical love inspires awe *and* demands action. Love requires sacrifice and long-suffering. It can't exist without patience and forbearance. After all, it's one thing to celebrate forgiveness, but quite another to loosen your own hands from someone's neck. It's one thing to desire family connection between believers, but quite another to care for a family's children because of an unexpected illness. It's one thing to extol unity and restoration, but quite another to knock on a brother's door ready to speak the truth in love.

Just as with the generator, you could ask: how does such love work? I could answer by pointing to individual acts of love. But a more basic answer lies beneath them. The church loves because she's been loved. The mechanics of true gospel community show that our love finds its pattern and power in Christ's love. The death, burial and resurrection of Jesus enable His people to love even when it's costly. His accomplishments on our behalf motivate us to live as He commanded. Everything He calls us to for one another's sake grows out of what He's done for us.

Gospel truth drives many of the forms of love we've seen. True forgiveness and reconciliation, for example, operate on this principle. We forgive because God forgave us in Christ. Our sin-debt dwarfs anything we will ever forgive in another. Released from such a burden, we ought to extend the same mercy to others.

Likewise, we reconcile with one another because God willingly reconciled with us. Just as the hostility of our relationship with God crumbled under the weight of the cross, so our enmity with one another crumbles when we stand before it together.

But the gospel also fuels our harmony as we rightly understand Christ (Romans 15:5). Service rises from the example of our foot-washing Lord, who even gave His life as a ransom (John 13:15; Mark 10:45). We humble ourselves because Christ's humility saved us (Philippians 2:8). When we give we follow the One who took on poverty for us (2 Corinthians 8:9). We love like family because His blood has purified our souls (1 Peter 1:22). And we love in general because of the hope of heaven, granted to us in the gospel God's dear Son (Colossians 1:4-5).

As the church looks back to the achievements of the gospel—and forward to its ramifications—it is propelled to live in holiness. The New Testament calls this a "worthy" life. "Only let your manner of life be worthy of the gospel of Christ" (Philippians 1:27a). "I therefore, a prisoner for the Lord, urge you to walk in a manner worthy of the calling to which you have been called" (Ephesians 4:1). "And so, from the day we heard, we have not ceased to pray for you, asking that you may be filled with the knowledge of his will in all spiritual wisdom and understanding, so as to walk in a manner worthy of the Lord" (Colossians 1:9-10a). Don't misunderstand the principle. A "worthy" life doesn't mean living in a way that merits the grace of God. Our lives never earn what God freely grants. *Worthy* describes a life affected by the gospel, not one that deserves it.

Imagine a large scale. A bar extends from either side of a center fulcrum—just like you'd see on a teeter totter. One side holds *Gospel Truths*. Precious doctrines lie here, like the incarnation and sinless life of Christ. Perfect obedience to the law, substitutionary atonement, and the resurrection weigh down this side of the scale. The other side holds *Your Life*. It's all the little things which make up your life. Your goals and relationships lie here. Your attitudes, words, prayers, and service all fall on this side. The side with *Gospel Truths* weighs a certain amount—but the amount isn't constant. It's determined by how much those truths have penetrated and affected your heart. If they're weighty—significant to you—then the *Gospel Truths* side of the scale goes down. The side holding *Your Life* goes up correspondingly. Your actions and attitudes rise based on how much weight the gospel has in your life. In other words, increasing holiness results from your reception of the good news of Christ. This is how our holiness works. Paul taught that our moral transformation comes as we behold the glory of Christ (2 Corinthians 3:18). The worthy life then doesn't earn the gospel. It is the result of it.

Looking back to the work of Christ grows us in holiness and love for one another. "In this is love, not that we have loved God but that he loved us and sent his Son to be the propitiation for our sins. Beloved, if God so loved us, we also ought to love one another" (1 John 4:10-11). Ours is always the second love. The first love is God's love to us in Christ. But ours is the second love *because of* the first. The apostles knew they must ground the church's life in God's love because it alone could forge the type of love Jesus required. The mechanism of the church, in other words, runs on gospel fuel. Paul commands the Ephesians with this in mind: "And walk in love, as Christ loved us and gave himself up for us, a fragrant offering and sacrifice to God" (Ephesians 5:2). Reflecting on Christ's work on the cross inspires and enables us to love one another faithfully.

The gospel also affects our lives as we look forward with a glance of faith. In the great "hall of fame of faith" (Hebrews 11), we read of heroes who were convinced of things not seen (11:1). They had confidence in future events—promises from God which hadn't yet come to pass. That's why faith was needed. But in Hebrews 11, the author didn't merely highlight faith in future promises. He demonstrated how such faith affected the lives of those who exercised it.

Consider Abraham's example. God called him to leave his country and live in a land promised to him. Out of obedience to God and faith in His promises, Abraham fixed his heart upon God's future blessing. Abraham looked for a heavenly city (Hebrews 11:10, 16). He saw himself, therefore, as an exile on earth. He sojourned in light of the future grace of God. His faith in God's future action enabled him to live distinctly during the sojourn.

It's no different for us. We live by faith, confident God will give us an eternal inheritance (1 Peter 1:3). We strive to live holy lives as we look forward to God's sure fulfillment of His promises. Paul says that, "For in Christ Jesus neither circumcision nor uncircumcision counts for anything, but only *faith working through love*" (Galatians 5:6, italics mine). Faith is trust. Faith is confidence. When we have confidence in God's faithfulness, we are freed to live faithfully during the sojourn. At the blazing center of our faithful sojourn is a life of love for one another.

And so we come full circle to the costly love that Jesus commands. What would cause a person to love like this? A look backward at the supreme love of God in Christ. God redeemed us by One who gave up the glories of heaven. How could we forsake one another to cling to lesser glories? We also look forward, and when we do, we see God has promised us everything we could hope for and more in Christ. We look forward and see an inheritance better than anything we labor for here and now. We see pleasures forevermore at His right hand (Psalm 16:11), so we are free to loosen our grip on the pleasures of this world in order to embrace our brothers and sisters in sacrificial love. The love of the church is a gospel-fueled love.

I can imagine someone objecting, "Okay, okay, but what if it doesn't work?" It will. The gospel not only fuels ongoing love within the church, but love also proves the gospel took root in the first place. I'm confident the gospel will produce love because God designed love as the barometer for our true spiritual condition.

In the Olivet Discourse (Matthew 24-25), Jesus used vivid pictures to warn of coming judgment. He told parables of virgins and talents and spoke of sheep, goats, and gnashing of teeth. But the most startling portion comes near the end. What Jesus left ringing in the disciples' ears was a test for final judgment.

As He assigned eternal addresses, Jesus explained why He welcomed the righteous into eternal life: "For I was hungry and you gave me food, I was thirsty and you gave me drink, I was a stranger and you welcomed me, I was naked and you clothed me, I was sick and you visited me, I was in prison and you came to me'" (Matthew 25:35-36). In the parable the righteous were puzzled. They didn't remember doing any of those things to the Lord. But Jesus clarified: "And the King will answer them, 'Truly, I say to you, as you did it to one of the least of these my brothers, you did it to me'" (Matthew 25:40). Those barred from eternal life were also confused. Jesus answered them the same way. But this time, He focused on what they *didn't* do for the brothers (Matthew 25:45).

I know those verses may seem to portray our efforts as a means to salvation (we'll come around to that), but please try to see a vital truth shining through those texts. What we do to the "brothers" of Christ, we do to Him. Christ's unity with His people is both startling and clarifying. Saul of Tarsus learned of this unity as he attempted to drag the Lord's people to jail. The risen Christ thundered from the blinding light on the Damascus road, "'Saul, Saul, why are you persecuting me?' And he said, 'Who are you, Lord?' And he said, 'I am Jesus, whom you are persecuting'" (Acts

9:4-5). Saul persecuted Christians, not Christ. But in the eyes of Jesus, there's little difference. The church is His body after all. A sin against them is a sin against Him (1 Corinthians 8:12).

So, there we'll stand before the Son of Man—the mighty King of Kings. Either sheep or goats. Destruction or delight awaiting us. And our love for one another—or lack thereof—will evidence our true condition. I say *evidence* intentionally. Jesus doesn't mean our acts of compassion save us. They aren't the grounds for our salvation. Instead, the righteous ones are *seen to be righteous* because of their acts of love.[18]

Other passages of the New Testament agree. James related faith and works, saying:

> What good is it, my brothers, if someone says he has faith but does not have works? Can that faith save him? If a brother or sister is poorly clothed and lacking in daily food, and one of you says to them, "Go in peace, be warmed and filled," without giving them the things needed for the body, what good is that? So also faith by itself, if it does not have works, is dead. (James 2:14-17)

Before you reach for the Tums, at least hear what James is saying. A person claims to have genuine faith, but he doesn't have works. These aren't generic works. They're expressions of practical love for a brother or sister in need (strikingly similar to what the King of Kings will look for on the last day, mind you). If a person's "faith" doesn't come with a side of love, it's a dead faith. It doesn't save. The presence or absence of love for fellow Christians evidences true saving faith on the one hand or false and hypocritical faith on the other.

A few years ago, my family and I moved to an older house in our neighborhood. As we began to settle in, we met most of the neighbors. Our next-door neighbors were especially helpful. Barb came over to point out the rhubarb and the plum tree on the side of the house. The yard had been neglected for years, so we knew it would take some time to see anything rebound. I pruned the plum tree in the fall. The next spring I waited with baited breath. No plums. I told myself it had to overcome the shock of pruning and may take another year before pumping out a harvest. But the next spring, although the tree grew, I saw no plums. As I write, I'm heading into spring #4. I'm hopeful I'll see something good. But if I don't, I think I might start to question the identity of the mysterious plum tree. Why? Fruit trees should produce something—fruit. The absence of fruit could mean a health problem. But at some point, it could mean this isn't the tree we thought it was.

The same is true for Christians. They're designed to produce something—love. It cannot *not* happen. The absence of love for a time might cause us to ask about health and nutrition. How's the diet? Is it being cared for and appropriately nourished? But at some point, we look around and say "I think it's an elm."

Consider what the author of the book of Hebrews says in this regard: "Though we speak in this way, yet in your case, beloved, we feel sure of better things—things that belong to salvation. For God is not unjust so as to overlook your work and the love that you have shown for his name in serving the saints, as you still do" (Hebrews 6:9-10). Immediately preceding this passage, the author gave a stern warning for those who once showed outward signs of true conversion, but then turned away from Christ. He spoke of the sad end for those who have thus reneged on their devotion to Christ. He then turned with confidence to those receiving his letter. Their lives—he was confident—showed the fruit of salvation. But what were the "things that belong to salvation"? The love they'd shown to the saints.

If you have no love for the body of Christ, you have no share in Christ. Love for God necessarily leads to love for His children. Of any book in the New Testament, 1 John serves as a clarion call for faithful love, which evidences genuine salvation.

John says that "Whoever loves his brother abides in the light, and in him there is no cause for stumbling. But whoever hates his brother is in the darkness" (1 John 2:10-11a). In John's theology light is God's saving Truth in the form of His Son (John 1:4, 9; 8:12). Jesus said, "I have come into the world as light, so that whoever believes in me may not remain in darkness" (John 12:46). Man naturally abides in a state of darkness, earning future judgment. He has no fellowship with God (1 John 1:6-7). His relationship to others makes his hopeless state known. Hatred outside means darkness inside.

Our love—or hatred—of brothers and sisters in Christ tells the state of our soul. John's entire letter drives this conclusion:

> "We know that we have passed out of death into life, because we love the brothers. Whoever does not love abides in death. Everyone who hates his brother is a murderer, and you know that no murderer has eternal life abiding in him" (1 John 3:14-15).

> "Beloved, let us love one another, for love is from God, and whoever loves has been born of God and knows God" (1 John 4:7).

> "Anyone who does not love does not know God, because God is love" (1 John 4:8).

"If anyone says, "I love God," and hates his brother, he is a liar; for he who does not love his brother whom he has seen cannot love God whom he has not seen. And this commandment we have from him: whoever loves God must also love his brother" (1 John 4:20-21).

"Everyone who believes that Jesus is the Christ has been born of God, and everyone who loves the Father loves whoever has been born of him" (1 John 5:1).

Our love for our brothers confirms we've passed from death to life. Genuine new birth begets new life. And such life is a life of loving action toward God's people. "But if anyone has the world's goods and sees his brother in need, yet closes his heart against him, how does God's love abide in him?" (1 John 3:17). If we love the Father, we will love the ones He's brought forth. John agrees with James. James agrees with the author of Hebrews. And they all agree with the King of Kings. A Christian's tangible, outward love evidences his intangible, inward new life.

CONCLUSION

"In this is love, not that we have loved God but that he loved us and sent his Son to be the propitiation for our sins. Beloved, if God so loved us, we also ought to love one another. No one has ever seen God; if we love one another, God abides in us and his love is perfected in us" (1 John 4:10-12). The love of God—poured out at the cross—lays a joyful obligation upon His children. They respond to God's love because this is what it means to be a Christian. God has designed for His love to be fully expressed by those who have been redeemed by it. Love in means love out. Love out means action.

CHAPTER 6

LOVE STRUCTURED

1 TIMOTHY 3:14-15

I hope to come to you soon, but I am writing these things to you so that, if I delay, you may know how one ought to behave in the household of God, which is the church of the living God, a pillar and buttress of the truth.

"It's like your grandpa always said, 'A job well-planned is a job half done.'" My great uncle reminisced about working side-by-side with my grandfather over fifty years prior. As he recalled those days, he smiled and recounted the old adage as if it had rolled off my grandpa's tongue as easily as *hello* or *goodbye*. Although I had never heard it from him, the saying summed up who he was and how he lived. When I told my grandpa his favorite proverb had been leaked, he grinned at me and said, "Well, it's true."

It is true. Plans enable cooperation instead of chaos. Drawings mark out the size and position of each part of a structure. Prints show how systems relate to one another. They direct the labors of subcontractors so everyone works efficiently. Blueprints make it possible to build and maintain a structure for the long haul. A job well-planned is a job half done.

With my grandfather's proverb in mind, I want you to think about the church. The church is called a building of God (1 Corinthians 3:9)—a temple comprised of living stones (1 Peter 2:5). Built on the firm foundation of Christ (1 Corinthians 3:11), the church is a pillar and support of the truth (1 Timothy 3:15). But remember, a job well-planned is a job half done. So what's the plan?

The Bible provides a simple blueprint for the church. To organize His building, God ordained three specific roles for Christians within the body: members, elders and deacons. When we understand the nature of each role and how they relate to one another, we can grab our tools and go to work.

But before we jump in, we must see that these three roles relate directly to what we've already learned about the church. The job descriptions for members, elders and deacons all aid the love of the body and fuel it with the gospel of Jesus Christ. In other words, the structure enables and encourages the church to do what God designed her to.

MEMBERS

Local church members have the most fundamental role within the church. Although the scriptures teach us about pastors and deacons, even they are members before anything else. Every member bears the responsibility to love, care for, exhort and encourage the rest of the church. As Mark Dever put it, "The responsibilities and duties of members of a Christian church are simply the responsibilities and duties of Christians."[19] The member's job description consists of four responsibilities: protecting the gospel, meeting together, extending communion and removing communion.

Local Church Members Protect the Gospel

Throughout the New Testament, Jesus' disciples are given the responsibility to exercise discernment in regard to teaching. In the Sermon on the Mount, Jesus called them to "beware of false prophets," and even gave tests for how to recognize them (Matthew 7). Paul began his letter to the Galatians expressing grief at their readiness to accept false gospels (Galatians 1:6-9). So serious was their responsibility to guard the gospel that he told them they shouldn't even accept him if he came with a different message. On the flip side, Paul commended and thanked God for the Philippian church which defended and confirmed the gospel (Philippians 1:7). Like Paul, John warned churches not to receive someone bringing a different message, because doing so would make them partakers in his error (2 John 10-11). The Romans were to identify and avoid those who brought teaching contrary to what they'd received (Romans 16:17). Jude appealed to the brothers to contend for the faith once for all delivered to the saints (Jude 1:3). And the risen Lord chastised or praised various churches in Asia Minor for their response to falsehood—praising them for rejecting defective teaching and warning them when they hadn't (Revelation 2-3).

These passages don't merely point fingers at a church's leaders—they appeal to local congregations on the whole. Every church member has the fundamental responsibility to help protect sound gospel doctrine. The gospel creates the church, sustains its healthy growth and fuels the life of love which ought to characterize the body. Yes, leaders play an essential role, but all members bear the weight of guarding gospel purity. We all uphold the truth. And when we do, the local church stands as the strong pillar God intended her to be (1 Timothy 3:15).

Local Church Members Meet Together

Although meeting together may sound obvious, it's part and parcel with being a church. The word church, after all, means "gathering" or "assembly."[20] You have a local church when Christians regularly and intentionally gather together. Simple enough. But I'm advocating a *commitment* to meet together.

From the earliest pages of church history, believers had a reflex to gather. The three thousand converted in Jerusalem upon the first preaching of the gospel immediately began to assemble. Luke records, "And they devoted themselves to the apostles' teaching and the fellowship, to the breaking of bread and the prayers" (Acts 2:42). From the beginning, Christians had an unflagging commitment to come together. Faithful discipleship necessitated it. Devotion to Christ meant devotion to one another.

But why such devotion? When taken in concert with the rest of the New Testament's vision of a local church, we see the regular gatherings as the primary setting in which Christ's disciples carry out their commitments to one another. The scriptures call us to love like family, to show care and godly affection for one another. Church members must edify one another as well as warn one another when actions don't align with the gospel. God's word exhorts us to sing together, pray for each other and instruct one another. And how can any of these happen if we don't see one another? It can't. Devotion to meeting together, therefore, is critical to a faithful church, and to faithful church membership.

God designed the church's meetings as an opportunity for love and fellowship to flourish. The author of Hebrews said, "And let us consider how to stir up one another to love and good works, not neglecting to meet together, as is the habit of some, but encouraging one another, and all the more as you see the Day drawing near" (Hebrews 10:24-25). In light of the Day of Christ, we need the constant ministry of other Christians in our lives, and we need to graciously give the same to them. This happens when the church gathers. We not only receive the love of the body when we assemble, we also grant it to others. But beyond that, we stir up love in them so the glory of Christ shines from His church. So, when the whole church gathers, you should gather with the church.

Local Church Members Extend Communion

By communion, I mean the love and mutual edification the scriptures call us to do. Communion includes intentionally discipling and building others up in Christ. Communion involves caring for, encouraging, exhorting and even correcting brothers and sisters in love. Communion treats the church as the household of God, exhibiting familial affection and care. Really, *communion* represents all that we've seen in the first four chapters.

Extending communion means one member paying the ongoing debt of love for others who have joined them in commitment to Christ. Paul's second letter to the Corinthians pictures how the church offers loving communion. Addressing a previous case in which he'd instructed the church to remove a sinning brother from their midst,[21] Paul now urged them to welcome him back into their fellowship by instructing them to "reaffirm your love for him" (2 Corinthians 2:8). Welcoming a brother back into the fellowship meant *re*-affirming love. Welcoming a person into the fellowship the first time then must mean *affirming* our love. The New Testament calls church members to extend this type of communion.

Local Church Members Remove Communion

It may seem odd to you, but removing communion is one of the most important actions a body can take. Earlier we saw that love means walking through difficult times together. Even when difficult times are brought on by sin, we must deal with them intentionally. When a brother or sister persists in outward, unrepentant sin, the church must confront it. The confrontation should be kept small and as private as possible (Matthew 18:15-17), but it must happen. If a brother doesn't repent, the circle of appeal grows. At some point in the process, the entire church learns about the sin to make a corporate appeal to the wayward brother or sister.

Sadly, sometimes even the weight of appeal from the whole body proves ineffective. When this occurs, the church has the responsibility to remove the person from their number. Jesus referred to this exclusion saying they should become to us as a tax collector and Gentile (Matthew 18:17). Jewish tax collectors worked for the Roman government collecting taxes from their fellow Jews. The society viewed them as traitors, and thus excluded them from the community. Gentiles were pagans and unbelievers. They had no part in the spiritual life or worship of the people of God.[22] The body of Christ removes the member from the life of the church and the communion that characterizes it.

One of the objections I've dealt with over the years when talking about the biblical responsibility to remove communion is this: it's not loving. Excluding people could never be the loving thing to do, right? I understand the objection at a surface level. It does seem harsh to tell someone they can no longer be considered a part of the body. But I'd like to suggest the removal of communion—carried out biblically—shows the most love to the most people.

First, it shows great love to the one in sin. God intends the removal from the body to produce a type of godly grief in the sinning brother—grieving him to repentance (2 Corinthians 7:10; 2:6-7). Paul envisioned this removal destroying the work of the flesh and bringing salvation in the end (1 Corinthians 5:4-5). Our faithfulness can prove the medicine of soul that kills the disease of unrepentant sin in a brother or sister.

Second, this shows genuine love to the rest of the church. Remember, Christ calls us to love the entire church. We have responsibilities to watch out for *all* of the members, not just one. Consider Paul's similar thinking: "Your boasting is not good. Do you not know that a little leaven leavens the whole lump? Cleanse out the old leaven that you may be a new lump, as you really are unleavened" (1 Corinthians 5:6-7a). That statement follows on the heels of his appeal for the church to remove an unrepentant brother. Our faithfulness to this principle simultaneously shows the greatest concern for the one caught in sin as well as the rest of the church which might be entangled with him.

Many Christians see their church involvement as a passive experience. It's not. As church members, we have important responsibilities for the health of the body. We must devote ourselves to meet with the church for mutual growth. We must guard the true gospel. We must extend robust communion to all the saints. But we must also lovingly remove that same communion if a member persists in unrepentant sin.

PASTORS

Churches can exist without pastors. Any group of Christians in a given area who are converted and committed to meeting regularly for instruction and the celebration of the Lord's Table constitute a biblical church.[23] But pastors—who are also called elders or overseers in the New Testament[24]—are as close to necessary as it gets. Consider Paul and Barnabas as they traveled through Lystra, Iconium, and Antioch. They went,

> [...] strengthening the souls of the disciples, encouraging them to continue in the faith, and saying that through many tribulations we must enter the kingdom of God. And when they had appointed elders for them in every church, with prayer and fasting they committed them to the Lord in whom they had believed. (Acts 14:22-23)

Every church was a church before elders. But every church needed elders. Paul's later instructions bore witness to this near-necessity. "This is why I left you in Crete, so that you might put what remained into order, and appoint elders in every town as I directed you" (Titus 1:5). The churches existed without elders, but elders were to be appointed because this was what remained unfinished. The establishment of pastoral leadership, then, is not necessary to the existence of the local church. It is, however, essential for the health of the local church. But why? Simple. Pastors man two crucial posts in the church. If these posts are left unattended, a local body of Christ cannot thrive.

Pastors Lead the Flock

I suppose this may be implicit in the terminology. Most of us think of a shepherd walking before his sheep. He guides them on their way and cares for them as they go. He employs his hook carefully, leading the sheep on to good pasture. There they'll be healthy and safe. Spiritual leadership accomplishes the same thing. Pastors lead and guide the flock so they might be healthy and thrive.

When talking about leadership and oversight, I've found that many immediately think in business terms. Leadership then gets boiled down to decision-making. True, elders make many decisions about the direction of the church, but their shepherding task also requires walking with the sheep in the midst of real life. They seek to care for souls as those who will give account at the coming of the Lord (Hebrews 13:17).

Think of the way a father leads his family. A good father makes decisions and charts a course. He does so with the welfare of his family in mind. Paul saw the management of the local church the same way. In fact, one of the qualifications for pastoral ministry was the ability to lead a family. "He must manage his own household well, with all dignity keeping his children submissive, for if someone does not know how to manage his own household, how will he care for God's church?" (1 Timothy 3:4-5). Paul even called the elder a steward—a person put in charge of another's household (Titus 1:7).

Whenever I'm teaching a group about pastoral authority, I use the picture of a pyramid. I draw the pyramid with a line across the middle and ask the group to place two groups on the pyramid—elders and members. In other words, what's the structure? Most put the elders on top, and the members on the bottom. I tell them that they're right. But then I flip the pyramid upside down. Before doing so, the elders are visually pictured as in charge. They're above the people. But when I flip the triangle over, the elders lie at the bottom. Now the visual pictures the weight of the entire congregation riding on those men. Yes, they have authority. Yes, they make decisions. And yes, God calls members to respect them and submit to their guidance (1 Thessalonians 5:12-13; Hebrews 13:17). But it's all for the good of those in their care.

Although we live in an age which decries almost every kind of authority, the scriptures view legitimate authority as a means for good. It's given to serve, not sabotage. Fathers exercise leadership authority in the home by God's design (Ephesians 6:1-4). God institutes governments as common grace on societies (Romans 13:1-6; Titus 3:1; 1 Peter 2:13-14, 17). And elders are given to churches to bring spiritual growth in Christ. In the words of King David, "The God of Israel has spoken; the Rock of Israel has said to me: When one rules justly over men, ruling in the fear of God, he dawns on them like the morning light, like the sun shining forth on a cloudless morning, like rain that makes grass to sprout from the earth" (2 Samuel 23:3-4).

Pastors lead the flock by both sound decision-making and by example. Peter told elders to serve as examples (1 Peter 5:3), and Paul instructed the Ephesian elders to *"Pay careful attention to yourselves* and to all the flock, in which the Holy Spirit has made you overseers" (Acts 20:28a, italics mine). Notice the order. Pastors must stay spiritually healthy themselves to lead the flock. Their maturity has a direct bearing on the maturity of the church. As Paul wrote to Timothy, "Keep a close watch on yourself and on the teaching. Persist in this, for by so doing you will save both yourself and your hearers" (1 Timothy 4:16). Elder's lives carry spiritual weight in the life of the church. They must be men who can say with Paul, "Be imitators of me, as I am of Christ" (1 Corinthians 11:1).

When our team of elders considers a new man to help lead the flock, we take very seriously the qualifications given in the New

Testament. We take about a year to get to know the man, delving into his marriage, parenting, finances, and doctrine. At the end of the process, we grill the brother on life and theology. Then we spend time debriefing. In the end, one question hangs in the air after all others have faded: "Can we tell our sons, *become like him, and you'll do well?*" If we can't say yes with confidence, then we can't say yes at all.

Pastors lead. They exercise the authority of the office and serve as living examples of maturity for the growth of the flock.

Pastors Teach the Flock

In 1 Timothy 3, Paul lists thirteen qualifications for a potential elder. Eleven of the requirements have to do with a man's character. Only two of them have to do with competency. A prospective elder must *be* many things, but he must be able to *do* two specific things—lead and teach. As we've already seen, the exercise of authority is central to the New Testament's vision of pastoral leadership. But so too is the ability to teach (1 Timothy 3:2). "He must hold firm to the trustworthy word as taught, so that he may be able to give instruction in sound doctrine and also to rebuke those who contradict it" (Titus 1:9).

The early church held teaching in high regard. As we've seen, the early disciples devoted themselves to the teaching of the apostles (Acts 2:42). The apostles were freed up to pursue this work by the appointment of deacons.[25] In the same way, Paul later held that some elders in the church should receive financial support so they might devote themselves wholly to the work of teaching (1 Timothy 5:17). Paul counseled young Timothy to devote himself to public teaching (1 Timothy 4:13). Teaching sound, Christ-centered doctrine is so central to the pastor's role that Paul could even refer to them as "pastor-teachers," denoting the fact that teaching is part and parcel with the shepherding task (Ephesians 4:11).[26]

God uses the teaching of local church elders to both form and protect the flock. Paul told Titus any potential elder "must hold firm to the trustworthy word as taught, so that he may be able to give instruction in sound doctrine and also *to rebuke those who contradict it*" (Titus 1:9, italics mine). Titus ministered on the island of Crete in a tense situation. Many deceivers taught falsehood for gain, and in so doing, upset the lives of church members (Titus 1:10-11). The Ephesian elders needed to pay careful attention to themselves and the flock (Acts 20:28). Why? Because Paul warned that men would soon rise speaking twisted doctrine in an attempt to gather disciples to them.

Years ago, a member of our church gave me three framed paintings of Jesus. One pictured Jesus with a sheep around His neck. Another showed him walking before a line of sheep—leading them to pasture. The third showed Jesus with a staff, fiercely fighting off wolves to protect the sheep. Pastors have a high calling. God charges them to lead in love and to teach for nourishment and protection. The pastoral role may not be essential to the existence of a church, but it's indispensable to the health of a church.

DEACONS

The church of Jesus Christ came into existence through humble service. The Lord Jesus took the form of a servant in order to die a shameful death on our behalf (Philippians 2:6-8). The church operates on the principle of service. After washing His disciples' feet—a menial task in His day—Jesus instructed them to do as He had done for them (John 13:15). Through love we serve one another

(Galatians 5:13). But the church also thrives through service. I'm not referring to the ministry of every believer. Nor do I mean to speak of the action of Christ. The church thrives because of the work of officially called and recognized servants within the body. The church exists through the service of Christ; it operates each day by the service of its members, but it thrives because of the faithful service of deacons.

The word used for *deacon* in the New Testament is usually translated *servant*, referring to those who work for kings or wealthy people.[27] Servants benefit others by carrying out a necessary task. But in three instances, our English translations render the word *deacon*.[28] Translators treat these occurrences differently because the contexts show them as something more than a general service role. These are specific and official service roles attached to a local church. Paul's greeting to the Philippians comes with a specific address to the elders and deacons (Philippians 1:1). Likewise in 1 Timothy 3, Paul discusses the "office of elder"—and the qualifications attached to it—but then goes on to deal with the same concerns regarding deacons, "*Deacons likewise* must be dignified, not double-tongued" (1 Timothy 3:8a, italics mine). In both cases, he attached qualifications to a publicly recognized office within the church.

Deacons, in this formal sense, do what every servant does: they serve to benefit others by carrying out a necessary task. Deacons, then, are officially recognized servants within the local church.

So, that's the *what* of a deacon. But we must understand the *why* of a deacon.

Although Acts 6 never mentions them by name, some understand this as the root from which the later office of deacon grew.[29] In this section, the church at Jerusalem already consisted of about five thousand men and was increasing (Acts 4:4). The practical needs in the growing church served as the impetus for deacon ministry:

"Now in these days when the disciples were increasing in number, a complaint by the Hellenists arose against the Hebrews because their widows were being neglected in the daily distribution" (Acts 6:1). The specifics of this passage help us see the role deacons play in the body.

Deacons Serve the Needs of the Church

As the term *serve* describes, deacons benefit the church by fulfilling necessary tasks. The church in Jerusalem had already proven their commitment to providing for the needs of their members (Acts 2:45; 4:34-35). Their robust generosity exemplified the unity and love Jesus commanded. But their generosity ran into a practical problem. How does generosity work within such a large church? What would they do to protect the ministry of love and care? Answer: deacons. "Therefore, brothers, pick out from among you seven men of good repute, full of the Spirit and of wisdom, whom we will appoint to this duty" (Acts 6:3).

We may not have the same types of needs in our local congregations today, but we should still express the same heart of love. Many needs must be met within the church for harmony and peace to continue. Children must be taught. The poor must be cared for. The Lord's table and baptisms must be facilitated. Filled parking lots and broken buildings require attention. And the widows of Jerusalem have been replaced by a new generation of seasoned sisters to whom God calls us to minister. In all these ways—and many more—deacons stand to meet needs and bless the church with faithfulness and grace. After all, that's what deacons do.

Deacons Serve the Teaching of the Church

The mention of teaching may sound a bit counter-intuitive. I've already said pastors hold the teaching responsibility within the church, so what part do the deacons play? I don't mean deacons *do* the teaching. Instead, they free the elders from the practical needs of the congregation so *they* might devote themselves to the teaching ministry.

The early portions of the book of Acts show that the apostles had a responsibility and desire to care for and oversee practical needs (Acts 4:34-35). But they also recognized the importance of their role as teachers. When practical needs overwhelmed their ability to meet needs *and* continue teaching, they turned to appoint deacons.

> And the twelve summoned the full number of the disciples and said, 'It is not right that we should give up preaching the word of God to serve tables. Therefore, brothers, pick out from among you seven men of good repute, full of the Spirit and of wisdom, whom we will appoint to this duty. But we will devote ourselves to prayer and to the ministry of the word. (Acts 6:2-4)

Every local church should have this same devotion to sound teaching. But every local church will also have many of the same needs. Elders who go about their work of prayer and teaching get questions about insurance rates, facilities upgrades, visitation requests, and potluck planning. As the church grows the needs grow with it. The answer, however, is no different than in the Jerusalem church. God ordained for deacons to pursue practical provision so pastors might focus on spiritual provision.

Deacons Serve the Unity of the Church

The Jerusalem church had a problem because widows needed food and the apostles needed to teach. But another problem simmered beneath the surface. "Now in these days when the disciples were increasing in number, *a complaint by the Hellenists arose against the Hebrews* because their widows were being neglected in the daily distribution" (Acts 6:1, italics mine). Seeds of factionalism and division began to grow. We know God desires the church to live in peace, harmony, and unity (John 17:23; 1 Corinthians 1:10; Philippians 2:1-3; see also ch. 4). Deacons—by their service—enable unity and love to continue unhindered.

If you picture the church as a group of sheep, imagine for a moment instead of wool, each sheep covered in metal. When practical needs arise, each sheep springs into action to serve and love others. But in so doing, they begin to grind against the other sheep—metal on metal. Deacons serve significant practical needs and thus take the rub away. Deacons grease the mechanism of love and unity within the church, and so enable her to shine with splendor to the glory of God.

BACK TO THE BLUEPRINTS

The purpose of this chapter is not to describe roles within the church. Remember where we began: a job well-planned is a job half done. I'm only defining the roles so we might see how they get the job done. The church should carry out the command of Christ (chapter 1-4), empowered by the gospel of Christ (chapter 5). So, how do these roles fit together to do the job?

First, let's think about members. Although I described four distinct parts of the member's job description, they could all be summed up under the banner of love. Faithful members in a local church extend communion to one another by prayer, encouragement and practical support. This *communion* is merely another way of describing their life of love. They meet together to express care for one another, but also to stir it up among the body. Even their discipline—or removal of communion—simultaneously loves wayward sheep, and the rest of the flock. And all the while, these members contend for the faith once for all delivered to the saints. They know that only the pure gospel can truly sustain the life and love of the church.

The work of deacons guards gospel unity and brings practical blessing to the church. But it also allows gospel teaching to pour into the body. Gospel teaching fuels the mechanism of health and growth because as members of a church learn well, their love is spurred on. Their ability to minister to one another and build up other members grows. Deacon ministry then serves the whole body because of what it enables within the body. Deacons serve tables so pastors can serve the word and members can go on serving one another in love.

Finally, pastors lead and teach. They make decisions which allow members of the church to simply be the church. Being the church means a continual flow of communion and love which brings maturity and Christlikeness. Elders also lead by example because they're first and foremost faithful members. Their standard of life is one of love and intentionality for the good of the body. They love with purpose and affection and even through conflict. And this serves the church as they seek to grow into faithfulness.

Pastors' teaching ministry prepares the flock to do what God commanded. As the pillar and support of the truth (1 Timothy 3:15), the church must be ready to shut the door to false gospels

(Galatians 1:8-9) and false teachers (Matthew 7:15). Pastoral teaching prepares the church for all of it (Ephesians 4:11-16). In other words, pastors teach so members can minister the truth of the gospel to one another. In their persistent teaching, elders outfit the congregation to do what God expects them to: faithfully minister the truth of the gospel and reject all error.

But pastors also teach because sound, Christ-centered instruction fuels the life of the body. When we remember the responsibility of church members—and that only the love of God beheld in the gospel empowers them to carry it out—then we begin to appreciate why teaching is so necessary. The power of love is pumped out of the church because the fuel of the gospel is poured in. If the church is God's flock actively caring and ministering to one another, then pastors simply feed the sheep with the nourishment they need.

Jesus promised to build His church (Matthew 16:18). And He chose to do so by assembling not just individuals, but roles they would fill. Those roles aren't a part of some archaic tradition which exists for the sake of nostalgia. They're God's design so His church might hold together in ever-growing love and unity because of His gospel. That's a job well-planned. Now let's get it done.

CHAPTER 7

LOVE GATHERED

HEBREWS 10:24-25

*And let us consider how to stir up one another to love
and good works, not neglecting to meet together, as is
the habit of some, but encouraging one another, and
all the more as you see the Day drawing near.*

Every Sunday I see people filing in through those front doors
Got a cross up on that steeple, yeah it's time to praise the Lord
Some watch it on their TV, sittin' on the couch
Me, I get in my old Bronco and point those headlights out
Oh, ain't got too many miles to go, to save my soul[30]

I heard those words in a country song one Saturday morning as
I dug and raked in my backyard. Most country songs don't pique
my interest—even with their vague references to Christian faith.
But this one grabbed me because it seemed to provide a snapshot
of our culture's way of thinking about church. Church is what

you make of it. Some folks like putting on their Sunday best and gathering in church buildings. But others find God on their own. Really, any place you can go to get away from it all and think about God a little will do the job.

But there's a problem in this steel-guitar-spirituality. "Me, I get in my old Bronco and point those headlights out." Did you pick up on it? There are no people involved. And with no people, this "church" ceases to even be one. Church isn't about you and your need to escape from it all. A church is a group of God's redeemed people intentionally and regularly gathering in His presence. As much as you might recognize God's power down at the beach or on the open road, you shouldn't confuse the experience with church.

God has ordained the church's regular gatherings as the primary means of carrying out Christ's love command. When we come together the gospel goes deep within the body. Brothers and sisters encourage and teach one another. Saints are equipped for evangelism and discipling on the Lord's day.[31] I'm not saying these things only happen at one place and time in the life of the church. God's people will do more than gather on the Lord's day. But they must never do less.

Let me do my best to argue for filing in those church doors week by week by showing what we ought to do once we're inside. Sunday best or not, these practices serve God's purposes for the whole body. So back up the Bronco and park it next to the parsonage for the morning. We've got five things to do together.

WE LEARN

We know the early church had an impulse to come together as a body. Their gatherings served as the primary setting for the apostles' teaching to penetrate the hearts of God's people (Acts 2:42). In words of pastoral guidance to Timothy, Paul counseled him to "devote yourself to the public reading of Scripture, to exhortation, to teaching" (1 Timothy 4:13). Just as the earliest disciples devoted themselves to the apostles' teaching when they gathered, so must congregations of God's people everywhere. But why?

We Learn to be Changed

The apostles' teaching held a central place in the gathering because they believed the gospel not only saved people, it would also sanctify them. Jesus prayed for His disciples: "Sanctify them in the truth; your word is truth" (John 17:17). Consistent teaching about Christ brings soundness in faith and increasing maturity. "Therefore, as you received Christ Jesus the Lord, so walk in him, rooted and built up in him and established in the faith, *just as you were taught*, abounding in thanksgiving" (Colossians 2:6-7, italics mine). Teaching brings health and growth.

This principle explains why teaching fuels the love of the body. Paul assured us that as we behold the glory of Christ in the gospel, the Spirit transforms us (2 Corinthians 3:18). When we see more of Christ's love, His love constrains us to use our lives for His glory and the good of others (2 Corinthians 5:14-15). The more we know His forgiveness, the more readily we forgive (Matthew 18:21-35). When we remember Christ's humility that caused Him to lay aside glory to serve sinners, the same humility takes a hold on us, producing service and grace (Philippians 2:3-8). Our learning serves our loving.

We Learn to be Equipped

Regular teaching on the Lord's day also equips God's church. God calls members of the body to teach and disciple one another. We must, therefore, sit under the preaching of God's word as much for others' benefit as for our own. Didn't Paul say that pastor-teachers did their work to "equip the saints for the work of ministry" (Ephesians 4:12a)? Just a few breaths later, he said church members "speak the truth in love" to one another (4:15). This truth-speaking was a doctrinal speech. It resulted in a person's stabilization against every wind of doctrine (4:14). We can't fulfill our ministries to one another without speaking gospel truth. And we won't speak gospel truth faithfully to others if no one has preached it faithfully to us.

In light of this, we can't view our corporate gatherings as mere passive times of intellectual learning. Pastors teach truth so members can speak truth. They give the gospel so the church can guard the gospel. They teach Christ so church members can ground one another in Him. So, how do you listen to preaching each week? Do you listen as a reservoir, storing up knowledge and insight? Or do you listen as a pipeline, knowing that God will mediate His truth to others through you (Colossians 3:16)?

WE PRAY

Pray without ceasing. Be constant in prayer. Go into your closet, and there, pray. Prayer is at the heart of the Christian life, and rightly so. Through prayer we draw near to God and commune with Him. In prayer we worship and praise. We confess our sins and lay our requests at God's feet. We also realign our hearts to

His will, endeavoring to pray in truth, "Hallowed be your name" (Matthew 6:9). Prayer lies at the heart of a Christian's life.

Prayer should also lie at the heart of a church's life. Through prayer *we* draw near to God and commune with Him. In prayer *we* worship and praise. We confess our sins and lay our requests at God's feet. We realign our hearts to His will, endeavoring to pray in truth, "Hallowed be your name."

Just as with their commitment to teaching, the early church modeled a commitment to corporate prayer. "And they devoted themselves to the apostles' teaching and the fellowship, to the breaking of bread and *the prayers*" (Acts 2:42, italics mine). Believers came together intentionally to join their hearts and voices in prayer. Paul instructed Timothy, "I desire then that in every place the men should pray, lifting holy hands without anger or quarreling" (1 Timothy 2:8).

But why should we pray when we're together? Can't we all just check that box off before we leave the house on Sunday morning? How does praying serve the grander vision of love within God's church?

Corporate Prayer Serves Our Unity

Paul called on men to stand in the gathering to pray. But note how he instructed them to do it: "I desire then that in every place the men should pray, lifting holy hands *without anger or quarreling*" (1 Timothy 2:8, italics mine). Corporate prayer serves as a weekly check on our spirits. Strife among His children makes prayer to the Father a sham. You can't speak with honor to the Father when you've just cut down one of His sons (James 3:9-10). In the Sermon on the Mount, Jesus said if a man goes to worship but then realizes his brother has an offense against him, he must pursue reconciliation before going on with his worship (Matthew 5:23). If that's true for worship at the physical temple, how much more as we enter beyond the veil? Corporate prayer acts as preventative medicine to our corporate conflicts.

Have you ever noticed that Jesus embedded, "And forgive us our debts, as we also have forgiven our debtors" into the Lord's Prayer (Matthew 6:12)? God has woven reconciliation into the basic prayer structure of the Christian life. We can't come to God for forgiveness—which we often need—without first being willing to forgive those around us. And don't miss the plural form of the Lord's prayer. We plea that God would forgive *us*. We forgive our debtors. Certainly, this prayer should drive our personal devotion. But it should also shape our corporate prayer life. As Edmund Clowney has written, "The Lord's prayer is a 'we' prayer, given by Christ to his disciples as a model for their praying together."[32] We pray. And the way we pray-if faithful-serves the unity we seek.

Corporate Prayer Serves our Growth

If you take a quick survey of the prayers in the New Testament, you'll discover the overwhelming focus is on spiritual growth (see Ephesians 1:15-23, 3:14-21 and Colossians 1:9-14 for example). But growth doesn't merely come from the content of prayer. It also comes by the practice of prayer. In 1 Corinthians 14, the apostle Paul makes an argument for intelligibility in the corporate gathering, saying he will refrain from speaking in tongues so others can say "Amen" and be built up by his prayer (1 Corinthians 14:15-17).

Corporate prayer allows many people to join together in mind and heart. The prayer of one brother or sister challenges and encourages others, just as if they'd sat down together and spoke from the depths of their heart. The one listening hears of gratitude and is challenged to be thankful to God for similar blessings. He remembers struggles present in all our lives and is prompted to pray for protection, encouragement, and steadfastness. Corporate prayer serves to both instruct and edify the whole body. D.A Carson writes, "Public prayer is a pedagogical opportunity. It provides the one who is praying with an opportunity to instruct or encourage or edify all who hear the prayer."[33] As the listener hears the prayer, he ceases to be merely a listener. The concerns become his. The prayer becomes his. And so too, the "Amen" becomes his.

WE SING

Redemption begets rejoicing. It always has. Those saved through the Red Sea under the hand of Moses sang, "The Lord is my strength and my song, and he has become my salvation; this is my God, and I will praise him, my father's God, and I will exalt him" (Exodus 15:2). John's vision of the heavenly throne room resounds with the responsive praise, "And they sang a new song, saying, 'Worthy are you to take the scroll and to open its seals, for you were slain, and by your blood you ransomed people for God from every tribe and language and people and nation, and you have made them a kingdom and priests to our God, and they shall reign on the earth'" (Revelation 5:9-10).

When we sing together, we direct our songs to God. Like the Israelites on the shores of the Red Sea, we sing of God's character and kindness. We extol His grace and magnify His mercy. Hearts affected by the outpouring of God's grace, respond with an outpouring of praise. Consider Paul's instruction to the Ephesian church: "And do not get drunk with wine, for that is debauchery, but be filled with the Spirit, addressing one another in psalms and hymns and spiritual songs, *singing and making melody to the Lord with your heart*, giving thanks always and for everything to God the Father in the name of our Lord Jesus Christ" (Ephesians 5:18-20, italics mine). Heartfelt worship overflows from souls filled with gratitude and joy. Our singing is vertical.

Our singing is also horizontal. Didn't Paul say that those filled with the Spirit would be addressing *one another* in psalms and hymns and spiritual songs? Our singing praises God. But it also appeals to His people. Our personal worship serves as a corporate calling to the church.

You've no doubt heard the common praise word, "Hallelujah!" Often, when I ask people what they think it means, I get the answer, "Praise the Lord." The meaning is right, but not the direction. The Hebrew word doesn't address God, but His people. Psalm 147 is a great example: "Praise the Lord! For it is good to sing praises to our God; for it is pleasant, and a song of praise is fitting" (Psalms 147:1). Notice the corporate context. The Psalmist *called for* praise to God. Praise is vertical at its core. But it's also horizontal. In our singing, we both praise God, and appeal to His church. "Public worship addressed God in the presence of his people; it also addressed God's people in the presence of God."[34]

But why should I care if someone else sings praises? Isn't that between him and God? In our privatized culture, it may seem so. But as Christ's disciples, we live and labor for a city on a hill. And the light which shines forth from the city emanates from the *whole* body of Christ. We all have a responsibility to work for the spiritual growth of other members, and singing helps them grow.

When Paul called the church at Colossae to love one another and let the gospel dwell deeply among them, he assumed corporate singing would serve as a means to both. "Let the word of Christ dwell in you richly, teaching and admonishing one another in all wisdom, singing psalms and hymns and spiritual songs, with thankfulness in your hearts to God" (Colossians 3:16; see also Ephesians 5:19). The gospel dwells richly in the church that sings of Christ and His work. With the Israelites and the throng around the throne in heaven, the church saved by the gospel goes deep with the gospel as they sing the gospel. When we sing, we glorify God, *and* we encourage His saints. Hallelujah.

WE SEE

Christ entrusted two practices to the church which serve as visible portrayals of His covenant. Baptism and the Lord's Supper allow us to see and celebrate the gospel and the community it creates.

Baptism

I got baptized at 22 years old—on a weekday. Because it was a weekday, only two others came—a pastor and a witness. I did it because I understood that baptism identified me with Christ and His death and resurrection (Romans 6:3-4). It marked me off as believing in and belonging to the triune God (Matthew 28:19). Baptism celebrated my entrance into the New Covenant. I had all of that right the day I was baptized. But I had something wrong as well. My baptism didn't just celebrate the New Covenant and my entrance into it. It also marked my entrance into the New Covenant community.

To be united with Christ is to be joined to His church. The church, after all, is made up of all those who have become disciples—those sanctified by faith in the work of Christ (1 Corinthians 1:2). Paul uses the language of baptism to speak of membership in the local church: "For in one Spirit we were all baptized into one body" (1 Corinthians 12:13a). As Paul went on to teach in 1 Corinthians 12, each member of the body uses his gifts and cares for the other members. Becoming a disciple means to trust in, follow and obey Jesus as Lord. And as we've seen, His foremost command is to love one another. We obey that command in the local church (see chapter 1).

Each time we baptize a new member of our church, we ask a few critical questions before they go under the water. They need to affirm their belief in Jesus as the Son of God. They need to confess their trust in His sacrificial death on their behalf. But the last question we ask may be the most uncommon: "Is it your intention upon coming up out of the water to live in obedience to Christ and fellowship with His church?" We ask this because at the end of the day, a person who can't answer yes to the church hasn't answered yes to the Lord of the church.

Baptism also strengthens our bond as a body. Just as the one undergoing baptism commits to the local church, so the local church commits to him. Other members witnessing a baptism don't do so as spectators. A new father doesn't witness the birth of his child with passive interest. He realizes—in that moment— the great privilege and responsibility of this new life. Likewise, church members cannot watch a baptism with passive interest. They must realize the great privilege and responsibility of this new life. God has called them to care for, encourage, pray for and disciple this new member of the body.

Baptism pictures and celebrates the New Covenant in Christ. But it also celebrates the Covenant community His death and resurrection purchased.

The Lord's Supper

Just as in baptism, the Lord's Supper regularly remembers and celebrates the New Covenant. In the New Covenant God gives new hearts and a new Spirit to all His people. He puts their sin away and satisfies His own wrath in Christ. In the New Covenant, we can know the Lord and walk with Him in joy, obedience and humility. The bread and cup of the Lord's Supper recall Christ's atoning work which secured these blessings. As Jesus said, "This cup that is poured out for you is the new covenant in my blood" (Luke 22:20).

But just as baptism celebrates individual blessing *and* corporate belonging, so the Lord's Supper has both personal *and* corporate implications. Our union with Him is the ground of our union with others (Ephesians 4:1-6). We are members of Christ and, therefore, members of one another (Romans 12:5). When we unite ourselves to Him, we join with His people. The table of the Lord celebrates that we've been woven together in Christ.

Recently, a member of our church shared a communion experience with me. She and her husband had traveled to see their grown daughter and son-in-law across the country. During their visit, they attended church with the family and participated at the Lord's Table. "It was so awkward," she told me. "Before they ate and drank, they all just stood there looking around at one another." I'm sure this would be awkward to experience as a visitor. I'm sure it would be uncomfortable having never done it before. But I'm also sure this practice perfectly captures the underlying burden of the Lord's Supper.

When Paul wrote to the church in Corinth—a church which battled much internal division—he called them to unity around the table of the Lord. He rebuked them for their lack of care for the body as a whole (1 Corinthians 11:20-22). And he indicted them for not properly recognizing the union which the Lord's supper

CITY ON A HILL

was intended to symbolize (1 Corinthians 11:28-29). He based his instruction on one foundational principle: "Because there is one bread, we who are many are one body, for we all partake of the one bread" (1 Corinthians 10:17).

The communion table didn't just serve as a reminder and celebration of Christ's death for the sinner. It served as a reminder and celebration of the church He purchased (Acts 20:28). The table calls us to rejoice in the New Covenant *and* in the New Covenant community. Although it may feel awkward to look around at other church members, the bread we break must always remind us of the whole body of Christ.

WE ENCOURAGE

All of the things we do when we gather serve God's great purpose for His church. Our corporate practices pour the gospel into the church, teach, equip believers and build up the saints. As a result, the church will live the life of love Christ called her to.

But we shouldn't forget the most direct statement about our gatherings: "And let us consider how to stir up one another to love and good works, not neglecting to meet together, as is the habit of some, but encouraging one another, and all the more as you see the Day drawing near" (Hebrews 10:24-25). The contrast to *neglecting* our meetings is encouraging and stirring one another up to love and good works. In other words, the church comes together to love and to encourage. When your feet hit the pavement on Sunday mornings, you're on duty. When God's people gather together, you have the chance—yes, the responsibility—to strengthen and embolden someone in their faith. You have an opportunity to help a brother's weakening hands take hold of Christ once more. You can love in profound but straightforward ways. And you can stir up the love of others. Jesus called us to love. And when we gather together, we not only love, we spur others on to love with us.

CONCLUSION

In 2016 another country song hit the airwaves. In *That's My Church*, Maren Morris confesses her failures to live up to God's standards. But then she explains how she finds redemption by getting into the car, turning up the radio—blaring country legends, of course—and driving.

> When Hank brings the sermon
> And Cash leads the choir
> It gets my cold heart burning
> Hotter than a ring of fire
> When this wonderful world gets heavy
> And I need to find my escape
> I just keep the wheels rolling, radio scrolling
> 'Til my sins wash away
> Can I get a hallelujah
> Can I get an amen
> Feels like the Holy Ghost running through ya
> When I play the highway FM
> I find my soul revival
> Singing every single verse
> Yeah I guess that's my church[35]

That's your somethin', Maren Morris. But it ain't your church. It can't be.

The church is the gathering of the saints. They come together in the name of Christ and for the glory of the Father. They gather every week because He's called them to love. They devote themselves to learn the word of God and pray together for growth. They sing with one voice, simultaneously lifting praise to God, and appeal to one another. They celebrate—in visible fashion—the gospel that redeemed them and the covenant that unites them. And every week, they gather to love and encourage and stir up others to do the same. That's my church. And with all due respect, Maren, you can have yours.

CHAPTER 8

LOVE DISPLAYED

1 PETER 2:9
*But you are a chosen race, a royal priesthood, a holy
nation, a people for his own possession, that you
may proclaim the excellencies of him who called
you out of darkness into his marvelous light.*

Not long ago, a friend approached me following one of our Sunday services. The themes of these chapters—which had been running through my heart and mind for months—began to leak out of my sermons on a regular basis. My applications called members to a more robust love and care for one another. The language of discipling and commitment crept into off-hand comments and prayers. She came with a question prompted by the slow drip of body-focused application.

She respectfully posed the question, but I could tell it carried traces of confusion and frustration, "It just seems like the focus is US, US, US. What about our responsibility to be reaching out?"

Maybe you've got similar questions at this point. Having worked your way through these chapters, you've heard Christ's call for us to love one another. You've seen the demanding nature of such love as portrayed in the New Testament. You understand how the gospel fuels such a faithful love. And even how both our church structure and gatherings foster its growth. But isn't this all a bit narrow? Haven't we missed the very mission of the church to make disciples and preach the gospel (Matthew 28:19; Mark 16:15)?

I chose the subtitle of this book for just this concern: The Light of Christ in the Life of His Church. I'm convinced that when we faithfully live as the body of Christ, we neither undermine nor neglect our evangelistic task. Instead, we empower it.

THE CITY SHINES

I speak of "light" because Jesus used it as an image for our self-understanding as disciples. In the Sermon on the Mount He said, "You are the light of the world. A city set on a hill cannot be hidden. Nor do people light a lamp and put it under a basket, but on a stand, and it gives light to all in the house. In the same way, let your light shine before others, so that they may see your good works and give glory to your Father who is in heaven" (Matthew 5:14-16). Disciples are light. But what does that mean?

From the opening scenes of the Bible, the writers of scripture associate light with God. In the beginning He said, "Let there be light" (Genesis 1:3). A close reading of Genesis shows that light came before God set the luminaries in place. He was the source of light. The closing scenes of the Bible bear witness to the same idea. In the new Jerusalem, God's people won't need sun or moon because the glory of God and the Lamb provide light (Revelation

21:23). John tells us that God is light and in Him is no darkness at all (1 John 1:5). And Jesus knew Himself to be the "light of the world," because He made God's character and nature known (John 1:18, 14:9; Hebrews 1:3). On the whole, the writers of Scripture considered light as bound up with God's presence, truth, and character.[36]

Listen again to the words of Jesus: "You are the light of the world." The life of Christ's disciples pours forth knowledge of God. Among them people will sense God's presence (see 1 Corinthians 5:4 and 14:25) and know His character. Remember, Jesus went on to say that in seeing our good works, outsiders would glorify God. That may not seem very significant to you, but just think it through. When we see a man doing something admirable, don't we usually speak well of him? But here, that isn't the case. We're God's light. Our actions represent someone beyond us. And when non-believers watch our life, they're learning far more about the nature of our God than about us. We're light. We should let our light shine.

Isn't this what we've taught our kids for generations? We teach them to sing about Jesus' words in the song "This Little Light of Mine." It's a wonderful reminder of our identity as light and our calling from the Lord to let light shine for God's glory. But it's not such a great model for how it should happen. The lyric of the song draws attention to the individual. But Jesus does just the opposite.

"In the same way, let your light shine before others, so that they may see your good works and give glory to your Father who is in heaven" (Matthew 5:16). One light shines, but it emanates from the whole community. In fact, we might translate Jesus' words, "Let y'all's light shine." The whole section shows that we, as the people of God, constitute light in this world. Our life together serves to show God's character and truth. Edmund Clowney, writing about the nature of the church and her witness, said: "In that witness we are not only individual points of light in the world, but a city set on a hill."[37] The collective image of a city stands in stark contrast to a strictly individual view of life and witness. A city only exists when people come to live together in cooperation and under a common rule. So the church shines when she lives in gospel-wrought harmony and under the rule of King Jesus.

In 1830 Charles Bridges began a book about the Christian ministry by saying, "The church is the mirror, that reflects the whole effulgence of the Divine character."[38] Together, we're light in this world. And may it be that when the world peers into the life of the church, it sees the very character of God shining out.

THE WORLD SEES

Jesus' "light of the world" teaching assumed the world was watching. They are. Quoting Jesus' words, Peter highlighted the very public nature of the church's life by exhorting, "Keep your conduct among the Gentiles honorable, so that when they speak against you as evildoers, they may see your good deeds and glorify God on the day of visitation" (1 Peter 2:12). Our life together is continually on display before the non-believing world. They will see. Their "seeing" may cause persecution or praise. But they will see.

In the early church, the thousands who came to Christ at Pentecost (Acts 2:41) committed themselves to discipleship. They started to love one another just as Jesus had commanded. They met together and prayed together. They shared meals and they shared possessions. And in this context, they had "favor with all the people" (Acts 2:47). Later, Luke reported that the crowds held them "in high esteem" (Acts 5:13). Non-believers observed the worship gatherings of the church (1 Corinthians 14:25). And Peter simply assumed outsiders would both see and ask about the life of the church: "But in your hearts honor Christ the Lord as holy, always being prepared to make a defense to anyone who asks you for a reason for the hope that is in you; yet do it with gentleness and respect" (1 Peter 3:15).

The world will see our life together. But just what will they see? The world must see the love of the church. The world will see disciples of Christ displaying His love. Jesus told his followers, "A new commandment I give to you, that you love one another: just as I have loved you, you also are to love one another. By this all people will know that you are my disciples, if you have love for one another" (John 13:34-35).

Disciples didn't merely follow a master. They didn't merely seek to learn from a master. They followed and learned from a master to become like him. "A disciple is not above his teacher, but everyone when he is fully trained will be like his teacher" (Luke 6:40). Our love for one another makes us most like Christ. When the world sees us sacrificing, bearing burdens, sharing in joy and sorrow, speaking the truth and resolving conflict with forgiveness and grace, they'll see our love. And in our love, they'll see His.

After describing God's love for sinners, the apostle John wrote, "Beloved, if God so loved us, we also ought to love one another. No one has ever seen God; if we love one another, God abides in us and his love is perfected in us" (1 John 4:11-12). You can't see God. But in the life of His church, you can see His love. There, His love is perfected. There, it's brought to completion. There, it realizes its goal in and through us. God designed His love to be re-enacted in the lives of all those redeemed by it. His love reaches its pinnacle not when it's received, but when it's reflected.

In a sermon some years ago, Mark Dever commented on his congregation's love saying,

How are we as a congregation reflecting this love? Do you know how Jesus said the world would know we're His disciples? Not by our evangelism program, or our snappy music—it would be by the love that we have for one another. That's how we will commend to the world what it means to know and love Jesus. Friend, does our congregation do that? It is essential to our evangelistic task. It is vital for our displaying God's character, and so bringing God glory.[39]

In his helpful book on evangelism, Mack Stiles writes, "I can't tell you how many times I have heard from non-Christian people that the church was strange to them, but what drew them into the fellowship was the love among the members."[40]

THE CHURCH SPEAKS

Seeing is believing then, right? Well, almost. A trap lurks beneath the surface of our discussion about the life of the church. Our love does show God's love. It does display the nature of the gospel. It does adorn the gospel with good works. But it does not *communicate* the gospel. In other words, the trap is thinking our living the love of the gospel removes the need to speak the gospel. Love is essential to our evangelistic task, but it doesn't define it.

Imagine for a moment that I have a flash of domestication and clean the kitchen sink and countertops at my house. Then I break out the steam mop and get the floors shining. Next, I organize the canned goods. On and on the cleaning goes. But here's the question: why am I doing it? Maybe I'm doing it because I've spilled something. Maybe I have an obsessive-compulsive disorder, and my mental health requires a little spic and span. Perhaps my family has been sick, and I'm disinfecting to stop the spread of germs. So, which is it? It's tough to tell what's behind my sudden concern for cleanliness.

Now, suppose my wife came home and saw the very same things I just described. She would walk over to hug and thank me. Why? Because she knows *why* I'm doing what I'm doing. Through the years, we've had many conversations about cleaning. And I've learned that helping out in these ways shows my wife I love her. Because of much communication, she can accurately *interpret* my actions.

The same holds true for the life of the church. Living a life of love does nothing for our evangelistic task unless we interpret our actions. Until those who see our love know it's an expression of God's greater love, they will not glorify Him. People will only see Jesus in us if they hear about Him from us. As John Piper has said, "There is no gospel without words. None. Nobody can be saved by watching deeds. Nobody."[41]

The New Testament shows that people come out of darkness and into God's light because they hear a message. Peter writes, "Having purified your souls by your obedience to the truth for a sincere brotherly love, love one another earnestly from a pure heart, since you have been born again, not of perishable seed but of imperishable, through the living and abiding word of God" (1 Peter 1:22-23). The "living and abiding word" is the gospel of Jesus Christ (see 1 Peter 1:25). The message of the gospel brings men and women from death to life. Through obedience to the *truth*, they might be purified of their sin. New birth, therefore, depends on communication.

Paul even identified those who opposed their apostolic mission as "hindering us from *speaking to the Gentiles that they might be saved*" (1 Thessalonians 2:16a, italics mine). True and saving knowledge of Jesus Christ comes through the spoken word. The good news must be proclaimed like all news. This principle has long propelled believers to the ends of the earth to herald the gospel. "How then will they call on him in whom they have not believed? And how are they to believe in him of whom they have never heard? And how are they to hear without someone preaching? And how are they to preach unless they are sent?" (Romans 10:14-15a). People come to believe in Christ only after hearing of Christ. And they hear of Christ through those who faithfully bring the message. Not in deed, but in word.

US FOR THEM

So, how would you answer it? "It just seems like the focus is US, US, US. What about our responsibility to be reaching out?" Does striving for biblical love hurt our ability to make disciples? Does the church's life together distract from evangelism?

Recently, a brother in our church had some hard luck with his vehicles. Bald tires, fuel systems and general wear and tear left Matt and his wife without reliable transportation. Working construction while his wife stayed at home with five kids didn't leave a lot of room in the budget to address the problem. But soon, others in the body caught wind of what was happening. Within days, a handful of other church members gave thousands of dollars to buy them a reliable vehicle and fix another. They did it because they knew Christ's command to love. And this was simply one concrete opportunity to obey.

Matt humbly rejoiced at the gift and praised God for the way He had worked through His body. But there was more to the story. Matt had not only worked in construction, but had viewed his job as an ongoing opportunity to speak of Christ. Regularly, he shared the gospel with non-Christian co-workers, telling them of Christ's saving work, and the joy of knowing Him. He invited them to know Christ and to come to the church's gatherings to hear more.

In particular, Matt had consistently shared the gospel and invited his boss to church. He usually blew off or flatly declined the invitations. But then the car problems happened. One day Matt needed to get a ride from his boss. The next day he drove a borrowed car. But then, late in the week, he drove another vehicle to work. His boss asked him whose car he had borrowed this time. Matt answered by telling the entire story of how a few faithful brothers and sisters had loved him and borne his burden.

His boss was floored, unable to conceive of a church so naturally responding with care and sacrifice. Later in the day, he circled back and asked Matt, "What time are your church's services?" What was the difference? Matt had always been ready to speak. But now, because of the church's love, His boss was ready to listen.

CONCLUSION

The New Testament never pits evangelism and vibrant Christian community against one another. It brings them together. The corporate life of the church gives evidence of God's character. More specifically, our life of sacrificial love bears witness to the greatest love of all. This is the vital bridge between our deeds and the great commission. God is glorified through our good works because we're ready with a verbal witness to Him as the source of them. People will come to salvation not because of what we do, but because of what we say about what we do.

Our lives are not the gospel. They adorn the gospel. And when people see our love as distinct from any they've known, we'll speak up and tell them that we're merely walking in love as Christ loved us and gave Himself up for us (Ephesians 5:2). Our lives make the gospel visible,[42] but our words make it intelligible. The focus is "us, us, us", *because* it's "them, them, them." We're a city on a hill, after all. And they'll see the light of Christ in the life and love of His church.

ENDNOTES

1 Hieronymus, and Thomas P. Scheck. *St. Jeromes commentaries on Galatians, Titus, and Philemon*. Notre Dame Indiana: University of Notre Dame Press, 2010, 240

2 Anyabwile, Thabiti M. *The Life of God in the Soul of the church: the root and fruit of spiritual fellowship*. Ross-Shire, Scotland: Christian Focus, 2012 pg. 237

3 France, R. T. *The Gospel according to Matthew: an introduction and commentary*. Grand Rapids, MI: Eerdmans, 1985 pg. 320

4 Deuteronomy 4:13

5 Morris, Leon. *The Gospel according to John*. Grand Rapids, Mich.: Eerdmans, 1995 pg. 562

6 Carson, Donald Arthur. *The gospel according to John*. Grand Rapids: William B. Eerdmans Publishing Company, 1991 pg. 485

7 Carson, Donald Arthur. *The gospel according to John*. Grand Rapids: William B. Eerdmans Publishing Company, 1991 pg. 484

8 Hammett, John ed. Dever, Mark, Jonathan Leeman, and James Leo Garrett 'The What and How of Church Membership'. In *Baptist foundations: church government for an anti-institutional age*. pg. 182. Nashville, TN: B & H Publishing Group, 2015.

9 Hieronymus, and Thomas P. Scheck. *St. Jeromes commentaries on Galatians, Titus, and Philemon*. Notre Dame Indiana: University of Notre Dame Press, 2010. pg. 240

10 Moo, Douglas J. *The Epistle to the Romans*. Grand Rapids, Mich.: Eerdmans, 1996 pg. 926

11 Bonhoeffer, Dietrich. *Life together: a discussion of Christian fellowship*. New York: Harper & Row, 1954 pg. 23

12 Carson, Donald Arthur. *The gospel according to John*. Grand Rapids: William B. Eerdmans Publishing Company, 1991 pg. 462; Morris, Leon. *The Gospel according to John*. Grand Rapids, Mich.: Eerdmans, 1995 pg. 548

13 Moo, Douglas J. *The Epistle to the Romans*. Grand Rapids, Mich.: Eerdmans, 1996 pp. 774-775

14 Stein, Robert H. *Mark*. Grand Rapids, Mich: Baker Academic, 2008 pg. 450; France, R. T. *The Gospel of Mark: a commentary on the Greek text*. Grand Rapids, Mich.: Eerdmans, 2009 pg. 385

15 Bonhoeffer, Dietrich. *Life together: a discussion of Christian fellowship*. New York: Harper & Row, 1954 pg. 107

16 Louw, Johannes P., and Eugene Albert. Nida. *Greek-English lexicon of the New Testament: based on semantic domains*. New York: United Bible Societies, 1989 15.43

17 Moo, Douglas J. *The Epistle to the Romans*. Grand Rapids, Mich.: Eerdmans, 1996 pp. pg. 311

18 Carson, D.A.; Gaebelein, Frank E., and J. D. Douglas editors. The Expositors Bible commentary: with the New International Version of the Holy Bible. Grand Rapids: Regency Reference Library, 1984 pg. 521

19 Dever, Mark. *The church: the Gospel made visible*. Nashville, TN: B & H Academic, 2012. pg. 41

20 Bauer, W., F. W. Danker, W. F. Arndt, and F. W. Gingrich, eds. BDAG. 3d, Accordance electronic edition, version 2.5. Chicago

21 Hafemann, Scott J. *2 Corinthians: From Biblical Text – to Contemporary Life (The NIV Application Commentary)*. Grand Rapids, MI: Zondervan Pub. House, 2000 pg. 88

22 Laney, J. Carl. *A guide to church discipline:*. Eugene, OR: Wipf & Stock, 1985 pg. 56

23 Bucer, Martin, Peter Beale, and David F. Wright. *Concerning the true care of souls.* Edinburgh: Carlisle, PA, 2009 pg. 1. Calvin, Jean. *Institutes of the Christian religion.* Philadelphia, PA: Westminster Pr., 1960. pg. 1023

24 In the New Testament, *pastor, overseer* and *elder* are three different terms that are all used to speak of the same office. See Acts 20:28 and 1 Peter 5:1-2. See Strauch, Alexander. Biblical eldership: an urgent call to restore biblical church leadership. Place of publication not identified: Lewis & Roth Pub, 1996 and Rinne, Jeramie. *Church Elders: how to shepherd Gods people like Jesus.* Wheaton, IL: Crossway, 2014. Throughout this section both elder and pastor will be used.

25 see Acts 6:1-6 and explanation below

26 Hoehner, Harold Walter. *Ephesians: an exegetical commentary.* Grand Rapids, MI: Baker Academic, 2002 pgs. 543-544; Wallace, Daniel B. *Greek grammar beyond the basics: an exegetical syntax of the New Testament.* Grand Rapids, MI: Zondervan, 1996 pg. 284

27 See Matthew 22:13, John 2:5, 9 for example

28 And sometimes a fourth, when Romans 16:1 is included (NLT and NIV for example)

29 Dever, Mark. *The church: the Gospel made visible.* Nashville, TN: B & H Academic, 2012 pg. 52

30 Eli, Mike, James Young, Jon Jones, and Chris Thompson, writers. Saltwater Gospel on *Fingerprints.* CD.

31 The "Lord's Day" refers to the first day of the week, when Christians gathered for worship. See Acts 20:7; 1 Corinthians 16:2 and Revelation 1:10; cf. Beale, G. K. *Revelation: a commentary on the Greek text.* Grand Rapids, MI: W.B. Eerdmans, 1999 pg. 203

32 Clowney, Edmund P. *The church*. Downers Grove, IL: InterVarsity Press, 1995 pg. 90

33 Carson, D. A. *A call to spiritual reformation: priorities from Paul and his prayers*. Grand Rapids, MI: Baker Book House, 1992 pg. 35

34 Clowney, Edmund P. *The church*. Downers Grove, IL: InterVarsity Press, 1995 pg. 130

35 Morris, Maren. *That's My Church*. Columbia Nashville. 2016. https://www.lyrics.com

36 Alexander, T. Desmond., and Brian S. Rosner. *New dictionary of biblical theology*. Downers Grove, IL: InterVarsity Press, 2000 pg. 644

37 Clowney, Edmund P. *The church*. Downers Grove, IL: InterVarsity Press, 1995 pg. 15-16

38 Bridges, Charles. *The Christian ministry: with an inquiry into the causes of its inefficiency*. Edinburgh: Banner of Truth Trust, 1967 pg. 1

39 Dever, Mark. *Selfishness*. Sermon, Capitol Hill Baptist, Washington, D.C, November 27, 2005. https://www.capitolhillbaptist.org/sermon/selfishness/

40 Stiles, J. Mack. *Evangelism: how the whole church speaks of Jesus*. Wheaton, IL: Crossway, 2014. pg. 64

41 Piper, John. *No Global Mission Without God's Mighty Spirit*. Keynote, Cross Conference, Indianapolis, IN, December 28, 2016. https://www.desiringgod.org/messages/no-global-mission-without-gods-mighty-spirit

42 Dever, Mark. *The church: the Gospel made visible*. Nashville, TN: B & H Academic, 2012 preface, xi